they came to play

garret mathews

McGREGOR PUBLISHING

stories from the early days of rock ...

05 04 03 02 01 1 2 3 4 5

Library of Congress Cataloging-in-Publication Data

Mathews, Garret.
They came to play: Stories from the early days of rock / by Garret Mathews.
p. cm.
ISBN 1-930845-00-6
1. Rock musicians—United States—Anecdotes. 2. Rock music—United States To 1961—Anecdotes. 3. Rock music—United States—1961–1970—Anecdotes. I. Title.

ML394 .M285 2001
781.66'09—dc21 00-065371

Jacket design: Antler Design Works
Design and typesetting: Sue Knopf/Graffolio

Published by McGregor Publishing, Inc., Tampa, Florida.

Printed and bound in the United States of America.

contents

Foreword by Bruce "Cousin Brucie" Morrow vii
Introduction by Garret Mathews ix
Country Joe & the Fish, Barry Melton 2
Johnny Rivers 4
The Tokens, Phil Margo 6
The Champs, Keith MacKendrick 7
The Seeds, Sky Saxon 8
Buffy Sainte-Marie 9
The Diamonds, David Somerville 10
The Flamin' Groovies, Ray Loney 12
The Kingsmen, Dick Peterson 14
The Joy of Cooking, Terry Garthwaite 16
The New Colony Six, Ray Graffia 18
Rare Earth, Peter Rivera 19
Jaggerz, William Maybray 20
The Grass Roots, Creed Bratton 22
The Fireballs, George Tomsco 24
Narvel Felts 26
Tom Paxton 28
"Mr Custer," Larry Verne 30
Sam the Sham and the Pharaohs, Domingo Samudio 32
The Shadows of Night, Tom Schiffour 34
Black Oak Arkansas, Jim Dandy Mangrum 35
Fabian Forte 37
The Cleftones, Berman Patterson 38
The Ides of March, Larry Millas 40
The Majors, Frank Troutt 41
The Playmates, Donny Conn 42
1910 Fruitgum Company, Frank Jeckell 43
Leroy Van Dyke 44
Soul Survivors, Richard Ingui 47
The Surfaris, Jim Pash 48
Sugarloaf, Bob MacVittie 50
Richard Gottehrer 51
Harper's Bizarre, Dick Scoppetone 52
The Harptones, Raoul Cita 54
Johnny and the Hurricanes, Bo Savich 56
Lemon Pipers, Ivan Browne 59
Frank Metis 60
The Association, Jim Yester 61

The Chantays, Bob Spickard 62
Herman's Hermits, Peter Noone 64
Mason Williams 66
Little Anthony and the Imperials, Anthony Gourdine 68
Ohio Express, Dean Kastran 70
Kay Starr 71
Ray Conniff 72
The Weavers, Fred Hellerman 74
Danny and the Juniors, Joe Terry 76
Sil Austin 78
Sha Na Na, Jocko Marcellino 80
Randy and the Rainbows, Mike Zero 82
Eddie Platt 84
Elephant's Memory, Myron Yules 85
Jerry Jaye 86
Captain Beefheart and the Magic Band, Bill Harkleroad 88
Holy Modal Rounders, Peter Stempfel 89
Spanky and Our Gang, Nigel Pickering 90
Blues Magoos, Peppy Castro 91
American Breed, Gary Loizzo 92
The Dubs, Cleveland Still 94
The Blues Project, Andy Kulberg 95
Cool Ghoul, John Zacherle 96
Five Keys, Maryland Pierce 98
Bruce Tergesen 100
John Marascalco 101
The Electric Prunes, Preston Ritter 102
The Regents, Guy Villari 104
Little Joey and the Flips, Fred Gerace 105
It's a Beautiful Day, Hal Wagenet 106
Paul Butterfield Blues Band, Mark Naftalin 108
The Nutty Squirrels, Sascha Burland 110
The Kingston Trio, Bob Shane 112
The Happenings, Bob Miranda 114
Al Delory 116
The Chimes, Leonard Cocco 117
Jim Kweskin Jug Band, Fritz Richmond 118
The Highlights, Frank Calzaretta 120
Dick Dale 122
Photo credits 123
Index of bands 125
Index of artists 127

To MaryAnne, Colin and Evan

FOREWORD by Bruce (Cousin Brucie) Morrow

It is written (somewhere) that if you remember the '50s or '60s, you weren't there. This is not quite true. It should read: If you remember some of the '50s or '60s, you WERE there. The mind is like an analog eraser (otherwise we would all be a lot more neurotic than we are) — notice I said analog and not digital. During those happy times, we relied on a real solid machine, not just a couple of "0's" and "1's." We had the whole alphabet and numerical system to fall back on. Today, what's a kid of the 2000s gonna fall back on — some flat-sounding digital "0's" and "1's." Forget about it! So the Cousin Brucie Theory of Irrelativity takes shape and you are now ready to legally conjure up those old images and memories once again.

I have read, discussed and written books and articles about those golden oldie decades. Some printed and some electronically driven have approached the emotion, the lotion and the ocean of those 3-D frozen moments of our youth. However, can you catch a star, a comet, that first kiss or that first touch? Can anyone capture that feeling in your belly when you scored your first bodily release (finally not by your own stimulation)? When he or she looked through you like

nobody else ever will? The mind's indelible photographic album is stored forever, just waiting for the right program to link and release a flood of feelings with graphics attached. How do we download this life information? Microsoft hasn't approached this project, Pentium XX is not on the boards yet, and even Mr. Gates is too busy to think about the profitable '50s and '60s landscape. So where do we go? How can we tap this vast memory bank?

Fortunately, this fellow Garret Mathews from Evansville, Indiana, (that's somewhere west of New Jersey, I think) has discovered the right approach. His laboratory of text, *They Came to Play,* is one of the freshest and most honest probes for unlocking those eagerly waiting moments. Those moments that Madison Avenue, Hollywood and television producers have been counterfeiting for years.

Finally, here is a reference source of images by someone who lived it and had the audacity to really remember. So get to it. No more wasting time on make-believe digitized, pasteurized or homogenized visualizations of how it probably was. Here is the good news. So check it out and feel good.

Oldies radio legend BRUCE "COUSIN BRUCIE" MORROW is the only on-air personality in New York to have a street named after him. In 1994, Mayor Rudy Guiliani proclaimed West 52nd Street "Cousin Brucie Way." The sign is directly across from Morrow's studio at WCBS-FM. He has worked in the New York radio market since 1959 when he joined the staff at WINS. He later joined the staff at New York's popular WABC, where he remained for 13 years. It was at WINS that he got his nickname. An elderly woman found her way to the studio with a request that wasn't for any song on the playlist. "Hey, cousin, can you give me 50 cents?" she asked. Morrow handed the money over and the moniker was born. Cousin Brucie was inducted into the Radio Hall of Fame in 1987. He was honored at the Rock and Roll Hall of Fame Museum in Cleveland, Ohio, in 1998.

INTRODUCTION by Garret Mathews

Sixth grade, Abingdon, Virginia. 1961. When times were true and Castro didn't have lint in his beard. *Weekly Readers.* Hall monitors.

Dodge ball. Watching Jennifer do the can-can with her petticoat and realizing it's not that important she can't throw a football. No teachers getting hired unless they score 100 on the Frump Index.

Passing notes. Passing gas and blaming it on Steve Heslep. Holding your stinky bedroom slipper against your younger brother's nose and not letting go until he admits he's a communist. Putting woolly worms down Johnny Lloyd's pants.

Safety Patrol. Gizmo Bordwine and David Hutton sneaking smokes. Earning a penny for every unbroken pop bottle you find on the softball field. Field trips to the sewage treatment plant. J.D. Morefield getting sent home for throwing rocks into the works.

Random checks for head lice. The festering odor from the cloakroom. Gary Crookshank flushing my red beret down the toilet. Draining the liquid soap from the dispenser in the boys' bathroom and replacing it with piss.

Hula hoops. Howdy-Doody. Realizing that not only can Charlie Gregory beat me by 20 yards in a 50-yard race, he has twice as much arm hair. No teacher getting hired unless she can prove she wears hand-me-downs from Clara Barton.

Saturday night. Roger Goalby's basement. Our first dance.

His mother is scared to death her son isn't popular.

She has reason for concern.

Roger's hobby is pulling the wings off flies. He also enjoys sticking pencils up his nose. Once he snorted during science class and had to go to the doctor's office for an emergency procedure.

No mom works harder to make her son popular than Mrs. Goalby. She's always asking if we want to build Erector Sets with Roger. Or go to the movies with Roger. Or go get buzz-cut haircuts with Roger. She makes cookies for us. Does our algebra. Doesn't tell on Gizmo and David.

Anything so we'll come over.

But this time the lady outdoes herself.

Covers the ceiling beams with crepe paper and the furnace with shower curtains. Puts balloons over the washer and dryer. Even wears a jumper and knee socks so we won't think she's a grownup.

I try to get out of going.

Girls are going to be there, and I don't do well with girls.

I'm shy, homely and have ears bigger than Sputnik.

It gets worse. From a female perspective, I have the reputation of being a "yuck."

Not a "yech." Not an "omigod."

But a full-blown yuck.

Since fifth grade, I have eaten disgusting stuff at the lunch table for money. I charge 50 cents and only make one rule. Anything that goes into my glass must be a food or a food byproduct, and has to be available in the cafeteria or a kid's lunch sack. No Gold Bond Powder brought from home. I even toss in a sweetener. If I puke, I forfeit my fee.

Mashed potatoes, meat loaf, peas, salt, ice cream sandwich, grits, ketchup — it doesn't matter. These items will eventually achieve oneness in my small intestine. Why not let it occur a little earlier and make some money in the process?

Vinegar and milk is a lethal combination, but I always tell the guys I wash it down at home like Pepsi. I don't like margarine either, but I lick my chops and rub my hands in mock anticipation when they smear it all over the green beans and jam it into the glass. The bluff works every time. Sixth-graders aren't very smart.

These performances are my only moments in the spotlight. I am ignored before 12:25 p.m. and ignored after 12:30. But for those five minutes, I am the early 1960s equivalent of Mister Microphone.

Sometimes a dozen or more boys crowd around the table, eager to watch my adam's apple bob — proof that, yes, the fool actually swallowed the peanut butter-laced hot dog that's been rolled over a mound of pepper so many times it has developed the same chemical properties. Occasionally, the gym teacher catches a show, announces that I have a commode for a stomach and makes a Rolaids joke.

I dream about Barbara Price. Blonde. Pretty. Dignified. Has cute little sailor suit she wears every Friday. Brand new pennies in her loafers. Wears her purse on her shoulder like the high school girls.

I want to be her boyfriend something awful. I'll gladly pay Cupid $2 an hour plus expenses. I'll even undergo experimental surgery on my ears.

But what chance do I have?

Barbara was in the hall the day Brenda Johnson gave up her lead role in the class play when she found out the script called for her to kiss me.

Barbara was there when Miss Dyer broke every Actors Guild rule in the books and canned me in favor of David Hutton, not because he had better stage presence but because Brenda said she would kiss him as often as necessary.

She knows all the bad things about my life. Forget being her boyfriend. I'm lucky she doesn't blackmail me.

Mom and Dad drop me off at 7 and announce they aren't coming back until 10 and for me not to bother to call.

I make my way to the basement. God, three hours. Even if Roger does his thing with the pencils, and Steve farts his brains out, and Gizmo gets busted for smoking, that's still forever.

The record player is on a bench beside the lawn mower. The speakers dangle from either side of the garden tools. The dance area is the space vacated by Mrs. Goalby's car and the picnic table.

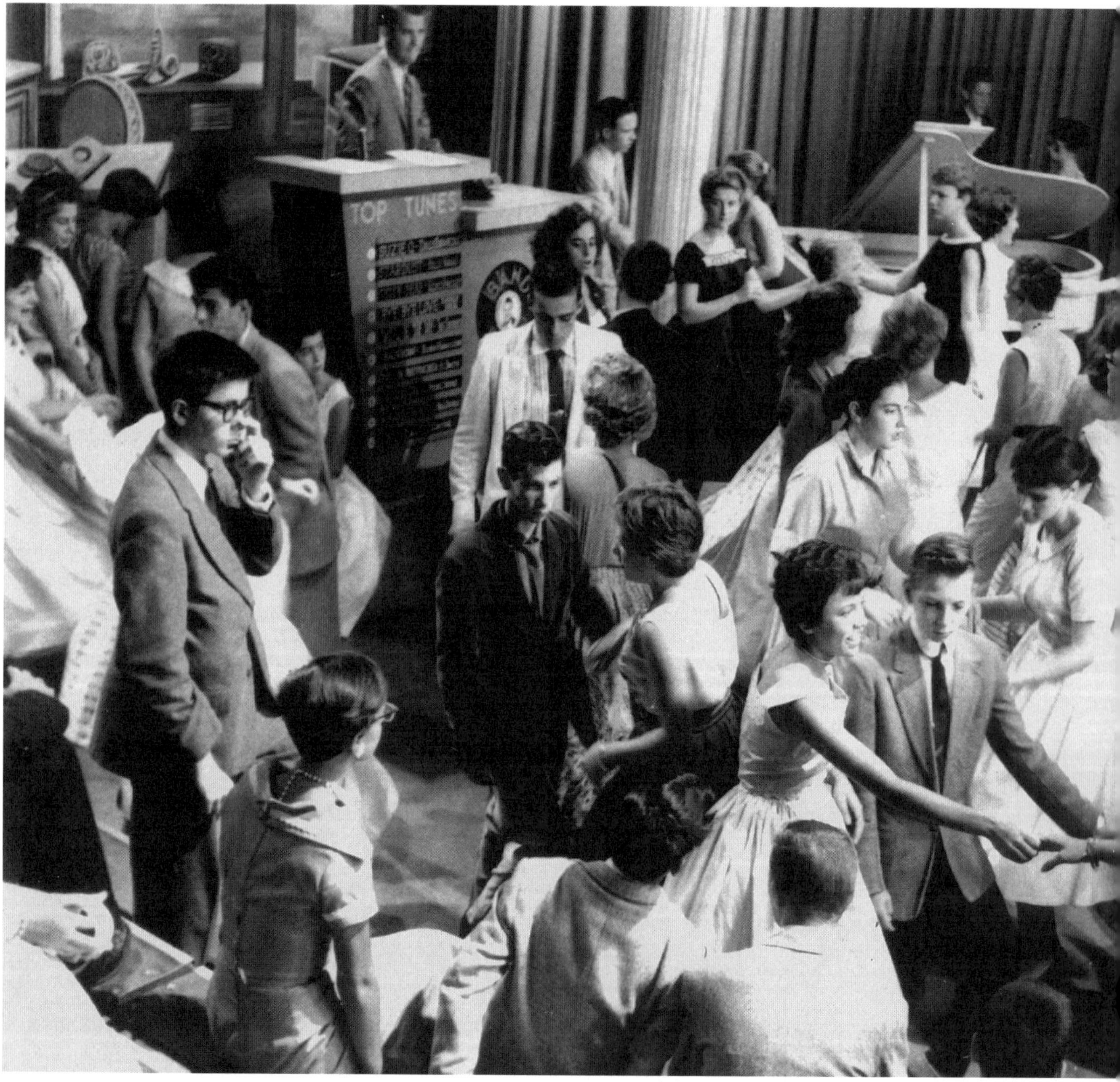
TOP TUNES

"Have a good time," Mr. Goalby says as he leaves for the Oddfellows Lodge, "but don't knock over my peat moss."

The boys gather on one side of the room and act, well, like 12-year-old boys.

J.D. threatens to hit Bobby Widener with a shovel if he doesn't stop talking about what happened at the sewage treatment plant.

Gary Crookshank tries to start the lawn mower. Tired of being ignored, Johnny Lloyd puts a woolly worm down his own pants.

The girls sit across the expanse of concrete, demure in their chiffon dresses, and conduct themselves like perfect ladies except for the occasional itching bodice.

It's this way for more than an hour. A siege without the ramparts.

Then Mrs. Goalby decides to play DJ. She puts on "Hello, Mary Lou" by Ricky Nelson. "You passed me by one sunny day . . . flashed those big brown eyes my way . . ."

Pulling down her knee socks because she says they're cutting off the circulation, she yanks J.D. to the center of the basement and makes him dance. Ten seconds into it, he falls prey to an oil slick. Laughter reverberates off the crepe paper.

Jennifer Jerrue, who has had a crush on Charlie since kindergarten, glides over to the boys' reservation.

For any other female in school, this would be an act of unspeakable courage. But it's what we've come to expect of Jennifer. The word is out that she's already kissed seven boys and has six more on her list.

Charlie, who can outdo freshmen in high school when it comes to suave, offhandedly tells Jennifer he is engaged in an important bit of horseplay at the moment, but should be available in a few minutes.

"Sixteen Candles" by the Crests.

"Sixteen candles make a lovely sight, but not as bright as your eyes tonight . . ."

Jennifer holds Charlie's hand in full view of God, creation and Mrs. Goalby. Then, more or less expertly, she puts it around her waist and they begin to dance.

The cutting-up ends. Charlie is the best basketball player in the sixth grade. If he's dancing with a girl, it must be an all-right thing to do.

Jennifer and Charlie are dancing cheek to cheek. Bill Sinclair, Bobby Widener and I watch. More than anything in the world, we want to dance cheek-to-cheek with a girl.

We're jealous, but also realistic.

"I'll never get a girl to dance that way with me," Bill says. "My glasses are always falling off my nose."

"My cowlick stands up too much," Bobby says. "It's like the antennae on Dad's truck."

"I've got a commode for a stomach and Charlie kills me at basketball," I offer.

Sensing the moment, Mrs. Goalby plays "Put Your Head on My Shoulder" by Paul Anka.

Bill takes three courage pills and asks Judy Shaner if she wants to dance. A miracle happens. She accepts.

On the pretext of investigating which brand of peat moss Mr. Goalby uses, Bobby slowly works his way to the girls' outpost.

Doris Jean Hatcher also takes a sudden interest in decayed plant matter. They meet. They talk. They dance.

"Will You Love Me Tomorrow?" by the Shirelles.

In the sea of chiffon, my eyes lock on Barbara and her little sailor's suit. Incredibly, she returns the gaze. I even detect a faint smile coming from just above the blue anchor.

I don't feel myself walking across the floor. I

don't hear myself popping the question.

"Sure," Barbara replies.

And we dance.

"Happy Birthday, Sweet Sixteen," by Neil Sedaka.

I whisper that I don't really enjoy eating horrible combinations of food. Kids don't pay attention to me all that much and it feels good when they do, I explain, even if I'm engaged in something really stupid.

Barbara nods.

"Sometimes I do dumb things, too. Today in English class I sat on the radiator and burned my panties."

I stop breathing. A girl has said "panties" in front of me. My right hand grows limp and falls. She massages it and puts it back around her neck.

I tell her I've made quite a bit of money swallowing stuff, and I've used it to buy baseball cards of my favorite Milwaukee Braves, and I've got 29 of Hank Aaron and 26 of Johnny Logan, and she can come to my room any time she wants to and look in my book.

She says her favorite athlete is Mickey Mantle, but she isn't sure what sport he plays.

We laugh.

"Tears on My Pillow" by Little Anthony and the Imperials.

She puts her cheek next to mine.

Mrs. Goalby hollers from upstairs that the party is over, and Mr. Goalby needs to bring his car inside really soon because it's getting ready to rain, and even more important than that, our parents are waiting outside.

Barbara and I don't hear. We're too busy looking into each others' eyes.

For that moment, at least, everything is right with the world.

I contacted pop singers and musicians who entertained us in 1950s and 1960s. You were in thousands of basements/dance halls like Roger's, I explained. And on millions of transistor radios. Tell me a story from back then, I said. The subject matter is up to you. Maybe a tale from the early years before you hit it big. Or the primitive sound equipment. The eccentric characters you worked with. The travel. The gee-are-we-ever-going-to-get paid. The push to be No. 1 with a bullet. The madhouse that was backstage. The monumental mistakes, or at least you thought so at the time.

Here's what they had to say.

Garret Mathews

they came to play

i feel like i'm fixin' to die rag

twelve kids from my high school were killed in Vietnam. That's what opposing the war was all about. It was such a tragic waste. Looking back on the late 1960s, I generally feel comfortable with what happened. It was an exciting time. A courageous time. And a stupid time. We did drugs too much and advanced their [drugs] cause irresponsibly, although if you put what we did in the context of time, it was more innocent than today. There wasn't anything sinister about it. We thought we were expanding our minds. Do people still ask me to do the Fish Cheer? Yeah, sure. We've certainly been stuck with that label. It's a wonderful, negative thing — a mixed message. That song shouldn't define me, but on the other hand, it did. At my age, to be known for something that happened when I was 23 is a strange thing. To me, Woodstock was a media event. It endures in people's minds because of the movie. It was a disaster triage type of scene. But it certainly wasn't the only place we played that wasn't well-managed. One offshoot of that experience was that it started driving concerts into large stadiums. I performed with Joe [McDonald] a while back at a benefit for a boy who was killed when a tree fell on him. I wouldn't say we were close. Money puts unnatural demands on friendships.

BARRY MELTON played guitar for Country Joe & the Fish, a psychedelic band formed in 1966 in Berkeley. The group is perhaps best known for the Vietnam War protest song, "I Feel Like I'm Fixin' To Die Rag." Today, Melton works in the public defender's office in Yolo County, California.

COUNTRY JOE & THE FISH

baby, i need your loving

I had a band in Baton Rouge in 1957, so I've been at it a long time. Alan Freed gave me a recording contract and changed my name from Ramistella to Rivers. I saw him for the last time not long after I opened at the Whiskey a Go Go in 1963. He died young. It was a shame because Alan was a great guy.

Why did I record "Baby, I Need Your Loving" over all the other soul songs that were out there? I loved the Four Tops and learned all their records. We were jamming on "Baby" one day and decided to cut it and see how it turned out. That turned out to be a very good decision. It was one of the first times a white artist had a hit with a Motown tune.

I signed Jimmy Webb to my music-publishing company and bought his contract. I had cut his "By the Time I Get to Phoenix" and knew it was going to be a hit, although for my purposes it sounded too much like "Poor Side of Town." Glen Campbell was a friend of mine and I gave him my test pressing of "Phoenix." It wasn't too long after that when I heard his version on the radio, and it really took off.

What's it like knowing I'll probably never have another big hit? I've had my share of appearances in the top 40. Besides, there is no such thing as top 40 radio any more. The biggest record-buying market is the over-30s. My songs are appearing in movies like *Austin Powers*, so it's not like the kids don't know who I am.

Louisiana-born JOHNNY RIVERS had major hits with "Memphis," "Secret Agent Man" and "Baby, I Need Your Loving" along with many others. He is still performing.

JOHNNY RIVERS

the lion sleeps tonight

The Weavers did a version of "Lion Sleeps," which was adapted from an African folk song called "Winoweh." Growing up, we sang it a lot on the beach.

But we were reluctant to record it because we thought it was too weird for the times. Everything else being released was "I love you, you love me" stuff. We wanted to go with "Tina" on the flip side.

Adding to the pressure was the fact that this was our last record in our deal with RCA. If it wasn't a hit, we were fired.

The Tokens could have been a lot more successful, but we were always doing different things. We never stayed just with the group. For example, we produced the Chiffons and Tony Orlando, and I've done a lot of writing and producing for TV. You measure us in longevity and we beat Elvis, the Beatles, almost everybody. But the Rock and Roll Hall of Fame? We're not there because everything is so political. You let the people vote and we're in. The Rock and Roll Hall of Secrets, that's what it is for us.

PHIL MARGO sings with the Tokens. Their hit, "The Lion Sleeps Tonight," was released in 1961 and sold more than 2 million copies. The group continues to perform, recently completing a tour of Major League Baseball stadiums.

The Champs was a great time in my life. I was young and ready to check the world out. We crossed the United States and Canada playing everywhere from big cities to Indian reservations. We even went to the Far East.

I had a band in Oklahoma City and my own nightclub. The DJ who promoted us brought the Champs in to play. Bob Morris was leading the Champs at that time and he liked the way I did business. That led to an offer for me to join the group when they left Oklahoma to go back to California. I took off. It was like paydirt had finally arrived.

Every time we'd go through a town we'd hustle the DJs into playing our songs. It was one adventure after another. When we weren't playing, Jimmy Seals and I were writing music. "Limbo Rock" came out and Chubby Checker decided to cut a vocal version. The deal was that if the tune was a hit, the Champs would be in Chubby's next movie. His version knocked ours right off the charts. And on top of that, there wasn't any movie.

I was a lineman before I got in the music and I'm a lineman now. That's 40 years and with a lot of fun in between.

KEITH MACKENDRICK played alto sax for the Champs, who had a major hit with "Tequila." Dash Crofts and Jimmy Seals were among the 30-odd bandsmen to be members of the Los Angeles-based group from 1957 until they disbanded in 1965. MacKendrick works as a lineman for a construction company.

tequila

pushing too hard

I'm a legitimate artist. I made the Seeds' music sound tight like the Beatles. They don't make records like that any more. It's like there's been this big sell-off in the music business. They pick the stars they want. They don't care about what it sounds like. I hear my music all the time in the movies. They've stolen from me all my life. You have to have big money to fight it.

The Seeds were a real band. We played our own instruments and we were one of the first to see the value of the piano. I helped bring the Doors out of the club-band scene by letting them open some dates for us.

Our "Pushing Too Hard" was about forcing wars on our people and imprisoning them. I consider myself an unsung hero. Bands are a dime a dozen. The movement is what's important. I helped usher in flower power. That's the greatest thing I've ever done.

We need to live organically. Eating red meat sickens God. Illness on the planet comes from eating meat. All my band members are vegetarians.

I'm the real thing. My goal is peace on Earth. My songs predict it.

SKY SAXON sang with the Seeds, a Los Angeles band that had a hit with "Pushing Too Hard" in 1967. He continues to perform with a variety of bands including Seeds of Sion and Dire Wolf.

the universal soldier

In the early '60s, students ruled. The cat was out of the bag. Ordinary people could have opinions and write songs about what we felt and thought, and actually reach a critical mass of like-minded people and change things. The government was insisting there was no war in Vietnam. I was a college girl marooned overnight at the San Francisco Airport, en route to the Purple Onion Coffee House in Toronto. The silence was broken by soldiers in uniform pushing terribly wounded men on gurneys and wheelchairs, coming into the waiting area where I sat. They said that they knew there was a war in Vietnam. In the next few hours, I tried to figure out who actually was responsible for wars.

Is it these poor enlisted guys? They probably joined the Army to get out of town and see the world. Are they responsible for war? Somewhat. Who tells them to shoot somebody else? Is it the career military officers who are dedicated to "making war better?" Are they responsible for war? Somewhat. Who points them at an enemy on the other side of the world?

Aha, it must be the politicians who actually declare war and make policies. Now I thought I was onto something. But who is it who votes for the politicians? Uh-oh, it's us. I wrote "Universal Soldier" in that airport looking at those soldiers, and partly in the air flying over the country. Basically, it's about individual responsibility on all levels of society: ourselves.

Canadian-born folk singer BUFFY SAINTE-MARIE is probably best known for her "Universal Soldier."

why do fools fall in love?

basically what we did was put a white face on a lot of black music. We helped bring R&B to a much larger audience.

We knew that Bill Randle of Cleveland discovered the Crew-Cuts because they were from Toronto like us. He was huge in the music industry and we felt if he could discover them, he could discover us, too. The Diamonds got a job in that town in 1956 specifically for the purpose of meeting this guy. It didn't happen until the last night. He liked what he heard and took us back to radio station WERE after the show. He played "Why Do Fools Fall in Love?" and said it was going to be a standout tune, but that it needed white voices. That was the first step down a very nice path for our quartet, even though it would be much later before we were in control of our recordings.

Do I feel we took something away from the black artists by covering their material? Not at all. We added to its appeal. I talked to Maurice Williams, and he said he'd be knocked out if we record their "Little Darling." Actually, his version charted after ours. I guess we owe each other lunch.

DAVID SOMERVILLE (second from right in both pictures) was the lead singer for the Diamonds, a white group of the 1950s that had hits covering doo-wop hits, most notably "Why Do Fools Fall in Love?" and "Little Darling." He continues to perform and stars in a stage show called *On the 1957 Rock 'n' Roll Greyhound Bus.*

THE DIAMONDS

slow death

a lot of people looked at us as if we were a famous band, but we really weren't. We were influential to a degree, but only huge in small circles. The *San Francisco Chronicle* voted us the fourth best band in San Francisco, and that's something to be proud of. People looked at us and said, hey, these guys aren't the greatest musicians in the world, but I enjoy listening to them.

We started out calling ourselves Lost and Found when we formed in 1965. The Groovies didn't come until about three years later. We played on the same bill with Moby Grape, the Airplane, Cream, and Janis. She didn't care much for us. We weren't bluesy enough for her. It's not real enough, she told us. Too much pop. She really had an attitude about that.

All the groups in San Francisco back then had their drugs of choice. Pot was our thing, but it was more euphoric than anything else. I don't believe it held us back.

Probably the most the five of us ever made in a night was $1,500. The critics and rock writers loved us for some reason. Some of them had never seen us play, but they wrote good things anyway.

Looking back, it was a great time, particularly for someone like me who started out as an actor. Our success always amazed me. I always thought of myself as an actor who sang.

ROY LONEY (in polka-dot shirt) performed with the San Francisco-based Flamin' Groovies. These days, he manages a record store and plays with a band in Seattle.

THE FLAMIN' GROOVIES

THE KINGSMEN

louie, louie

The group got started in the late 1950s with bongo drums and folk music. I came around in 1963 when they had more of a Ventures sound. I was in the high school library with Norm's [Sundholm, the bass player] girlfriend. She told me the band was being rearranged because some guys were going into the military, and that I should try out for drummer. The group was making $20 a week playing at grocery store openings, and that was good money, so I said, sure. I later learned I got the job because I played louder than anybody else.

[Lead singer] Lynn Eaton's dad heard about a cruise line that liked our music, so he paid $36 for an hour at a recording studio. "Louie" was one of four songs we sang and the only one we did twice. The first time, they said the vocal was too loud. The conditions were pretty primitive. The engineer couldn't change the mix, so all they could do was move the microphone up. You had less vocal and more junk, but that's the version that was put out. There were mistakes in the guitar parts, but we figured it didn't make any difference because nobody would ever hear it.

Then the FBI stepped in and said the dirty lyrics were corrupting America' s youth, and that's when we had a hit. The song was banned in January of 1964 and two months later, it was up to No. 2. You tell people they can't buy a record and that's exactly what they're going to do.

"Louie" was just a Jamaican sailing song. Some of the words were hard to understand because of the way it was recorded. We were just a bunch of kids. No drugs. No drinking. We weren't trying to pull anything over on anybody. Besides, art doesn't lead a people. It's a reflection of the people.

It was hilarious having the FBI on your case. They followed us and sat in on our shows. Spot 'em a mile away. The only ones in black suits. They started a rumor that we played in Saran Wrap and jockstraps. And this from a man [J. Edgar Hoover] who went around in a dress.

We were finally unbanned when a judge ruled

that "Louie" was unintelligible at any speed. What got us in trouble in the mid-1960s would be nothing compared to the music of today. I believe in freedom of speech, but not in language that insults people. Some of the music creates less respect for humans. You can say a lot and make your point without going all the way to the wall.

DICK PETERSON played drums for the Kingsmen, whose "Louie, Louie" may be rock's most infamous recording.

mockingbird

The Joy of Cooking played to celebrate the planting of People's Park in Berkeley, California, before the cyclone fence was put around it. We had drums, congas, keyboard, guitar and vocals on the makeshift stage on the back of a truck. The sound was energized by a generator, and somehow only one Fender Reverb amp would work through the sound system. That's a lot of sound squeezed through two 12-inch speakers, but the spirit was high and the park literally hummed.

In 1969, we shared the bill with my heroes, The Band. Albert Grossman shouted, "Get them off the stage," during our second encore at the Brooklyn Academy of Music. Later that year, we played at the Family Dog, a San Francisco rock hall, with naked dancers from the audience coming on the stage.

In 1970, I remember jumping off the stage in Salt Lake City to prowl through the audience singing "Mockingbird" while the audience sat on their hands. Also that year, I arrived in Michigan to play a benefit concert with John Lennon and Yoko Ono, only to be told that some of our band members missed the plane and we wouldn't be able to play.

When I was with Joy of Cooking, people used to tell me excitedly how much they loved the music because it was so great to do housework to. I tried it once. I can't hear bloody hell when I'm vacuuming.

TERRY GARTHWAITE (inset and second from left) fronted Joy of Cooking, a folk-rock band that had a hit with "Mockingbird."

THE JOY OF COOKING

THE NEW COLONY SIX

We were all attending St. Patrick High School when the British invasion hit in 1964. We had the idea of bringing rock and roll back to America, so we started calling ourselves the Patsmen, which eventually grew into the New Colony Six.

We were a straight-arrow band and, looking back, I really appreciated that. We liked to make music, we made a few bucks and we were sober all the time. I get tired of the VH-1 thing when you can't get on the program unless you had this or that addiction.

We eventually had million-sellers with "I Will Always Think of You" and "Things I'd Like to Say," but our distribution really stunk. We could have been in the top 5, but we never had that big thrust. We'd be big in St. Louis, but absolutely nowhere in Texas. Somebody figured it up and said we had 198 weeks on the national charts, and that's something to be proud of, even though the royalties I get are about enough to buy a Quarter Pounder with cheese.

The breakup of the band followed a progression that began in 1967. We had a meeting in which everybody in the group had to make a statement about the future. We were all attending college. Did we want to keep recording and touring along with going to class?

We had a few original members drop out over that. I was still in the band in 1969, but we had no kick-butt tune after "Things." I decided that going to college full-time was my best option. I had my fun with the music, but it was over. I've never regretted that decision.

i will always think of you

RAY GRAFFIA was a member of the New Colony Six. These days, he's in the industrial wastewater business.

NARVEL FELTS

TOM PAXTON

the last thing on my mind

One day in the autumn of 1960, shortly after my discharge from the Army, I was sitting in the Gaslight Café in Greenwich Village when John Stauber, a classical guitarist who accompanied the folksinger Leon Bibb, came in and told me I ought to audition for the Chad Mitchell Trio. One of the original members had left to go back to school and they needed a replacement.

I went to the auditions across the street from Carnegie Hall. There were scads of singers there, holding sheet music and looking quite professional. I don't remember just why, but I didn't even have a guitar with me. When I was called, I borrowed one from Roger McGuinn and sang something—I can't remember what. Milt Okun was the musical director for the Trio. He asked me If I could sing a bit of "Jamaican Farewell."

I could.

"You'll do," Milt said, and told an assistant to thank the rest of the people. He explained that they were taking me provisionally. We'd rehearse for a week and see how things went.

Obviously, they hoped things would go well, but, sadly it wasn't to be. At the end of the week, Milt had to tell me that my voice just didn't blend well enough with Chad's and Mike's [Kobluk, the other member of the Trio].

Devastation.

On the other hand, I had sung "The Marvelous Toy"—a song I had written during typing class at Fort Dix, New Jersey, when I was still in the Army—for the Trio during a break about mid-week. They loved it and said they wanted to record it. More importantly, Milt liked the song a lot and said—as he broke the bad news about having to let me go—that he'd like to publish it and that he'd love to hear anything I wrote in the future.

This was the moment for me that I wish for everyone who ever dares to write a song. It was validation, my seat on the bus. I was a songwriter.

TOM PAXTON came to prominence during the early-1960s Greenwich Village folk revival. Among his songs are "Talking Vietnam Pot Luck Blues" and "The Last Thing on My Mind."

mr. custer

I was working as a photographer in Los Angeles across from the Gold Star Recording Studio. I would eat lunch with three of the songwriters who worked there — Fred Darian, Al Delory and Joe Van Winkle. They were working on this tune about the battle at the Little Big Horn. I'd stick my head in the door and throw out a line or two about how the arrows were whizzing around, and how some of the soldiers might not have been all that brave. We finally put the song together, and they thought I should sing it because it was funnier with my Southern-sounding drawl, even though I'm from Minnesota. The first dub was awful, but we stayed with it. Eighteen hours and 20 takes later, we had it done.

"Custer" came out at No. 65 and it was in the top 10 five weeks before it passed "Chain Gang" and took over No. 1. We came out with another song called "Mr. Livingston," but it didn't do very well. The three writers managed me and put together a tour. I was thrilled with the success of the record and enjoyed meeting the people, but the road was not a fun place. It became a grind and I stopped after four years.

Altogether, the song made the four of us around $60,000. A pittance, when you think about it. I found out that I could make more with the movies. I started out as a stunt man, and then I became a carpenter and built sets. I've been retired for a couple of years.

LARRY VERNE recorded the novelty record, "Mr. Custer," in 1960. It rose to No. 1.

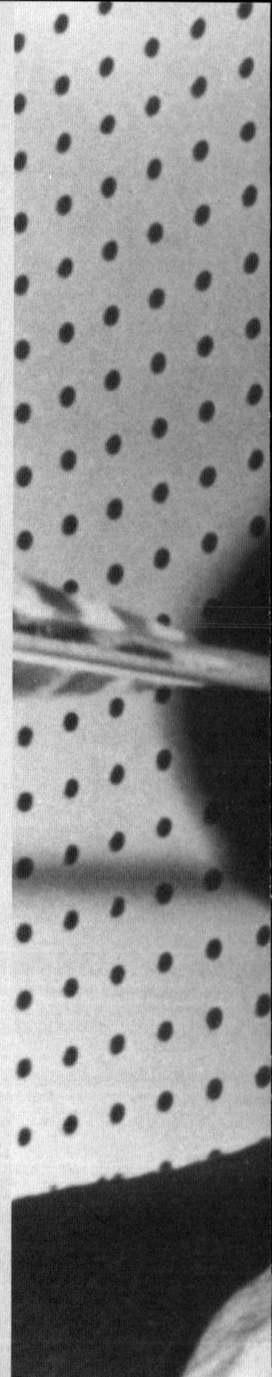

45 R.P.M
ERA
RECORDS

SAM THE SHAM & THE PHARAOHS

little red riding hood

I don't go as Sam any more. That doesn't mean I'm through with music, though. I have my own studio and I've been archiving my material to make sure they're recorded the way I want them to be. I work four or five times a year at family concerts. If children aren't allowed to attend, then I don't perform.

These days I try to serve others as much as possible. Give something back. I go abroad with medical teams to nations that have a lot of problems. Every doctor, pharmacist and dentist pays his own way. They set up a clinic for a week and see hundreds of patients. The way I look at it, "Wooly Bully" gave me a lot of opportunities to do for others.

Back then, I was someone who played by the rules. "Wooly Bully" came out during a very troubled time in our country's history. There was a lot of protesting, which our band wasn't doing. It was just an innocent little song and it wasn't bad at all.

I see what's going on in the country now and I'm saddened. If we're not careful, we'll fall asleep at the wheel. There's so much madness, but there's no panic in heaven. When God speaks, Merrill Lynch listens.

DOMINGO "SAM" SAMUDIO (on keyboard) fronted the Dallas-based Sam the Sham and the Pharaohs. The band's top sellers were "Wooly Bully" in 1965 and "Little Red Riding Hood" a year later.

gloria

I started with the band in 1963 when I was still in high school. I played for the love of the music. When it got to be a business, that's when it came to be a real drag. Our management put us out on 25 one-nighters a month and we had to drive 300 miles between shows. Lots of times we didn't even know where we were. We had to use other people's equipment and that was a joke. We were up all the time and for food, we'd empty out the vending machines at some gas station. Basically, we were killing ourselves. When I finally did come home, Mom would look at me and say, "You look awful. What's going on?"

College gigs paid the most — around $2,000 — but the frats had a lot of drunks and things got nasty. The guys in the group had long hair and that got us in trouble. You go in the streets and people would make fun of you. When we played at redneck places, we even had to hire a bouncer. We had to talk up the DJs and do a lot of freebies. I had no stomach at all for the PR thing.

We heard about Van Morrison's "Gloria" before other bands because we hung out at this Arlington Heights [Illinois] record store, and were always getting the latest 45s from England. We walked around carrying these big boxes. We liked "Gloria," but it was our B side to something called "Here Comes the Night."

My father was a big-band drummer in the 1930s and I grew up with jazz. None of our music was that hard. Usually three chords. A little floating type of thing that lasted for three minutes.

I was the first to quit in the late 1960s. I had a serious encounter with God and that changed the way I looked at things. I play at the synagogue or at prom parties, but that's it.

The Shadows of Knight are considered this big underground band. I get sent a lot of things to sign and I do it. I might as well be a nice guy about it. Thirty years later, I don't look at the group as any big deal. It was just something I did as a kid.

TOM SCHIFFOUR was the drummer for The Shadows of Knight.

My daddy gave me that nickname [Dandy] when I was 9. I was the first long-hair in Arkansas, and you throw in that Dandy stuff and I was in one fight after another. My sister had the talent in the family, but she didn't have the will like I did. We were out doing 300 dates a year plus two albums. Our management gave us free dope to keep us going. We were stoned as hell.

We couldn't get "Hot and Nasty" played on the radio. It was a joke song, but everybody took it seriously. It would be nothing compared to what's released today, but back then it got me questioned in Washington for trying to incite the insurrection. Hell, we might have broken a guitar or a washboard every now and again, but that was all.

The essence of Dandyism is to be remembered well because that's how you earn your hereafter. When you look at it, we're just a dirt clod in the sky. Why have nationalism? Why possess anything? Money just gets in the way. Rock is a vehicle, a weapon. The pen might be mightier than the sword, but watch out for that guitar.

JIM "DANDY" MANGRUM continues to perform with Black Oak Arkansas. Their controversial "Hot and Nasty" was released in 1969.

hot and nasty

FABIAN

turn me loose

I was signed by Chancellor Records in a case of mistaken identity. I was on the front stoop of our house watching my sick father being taken out by ambulance. The record guy drove by, thought I was somebody he knew and asked if I wanted to be in the rock and roll business. I blew him off because I was worried about my dad. I also worried about our household not having enough money. At the time, I was making $6 a week delivering packages for the pharmacy.

I don't know what the man saw in me. I had this butch haircut because we couldn't afford to get it cut any other way. He kept after me, even after he realized I wasn't who he thought I was. I rebuffed him again, but then my dad started getting better and I thought maybe music would help us make a better living.

I got "Turn Me Loose" from Doc Pomus and Mort Shuman. I flipped out when Doc first sang it for me. I wondered why he didn't record it since it was his baby. But they kept saying it would be better for me. I don't remember exactly which lyrics were changed, but they did move a few words around because they thought the original song sounded too adult for a 15-year-old to be singing.

Fabian, born FABIAN FORTE, was one of the top late 1950s Philadelphia teen idols. He had hits with "Tiger" and "Turn Me Loose." He's still out on the road.

It seemed like everybody and his brother had a singing group back in the '50s. I think we caught on because we didn't have that stereotypical rhythm-and-blues sound. We were a gathering of the various styles of that time—a conglomeration, if you will. Something bouncing and refreshing. Once you became popular, you were expected to work. I can remember playing five shows a night at the Apollo Theater. We went on every hour and were paid $500 to split five ways.

In 1956, the Cleftones were one of the artists, along with Chuck Berry, Frankie Lymon and Della Reese, selected to go on a big tour of the South. It was my first real encounter with hard-core racism. Our bus driver, who was white, stopped at the Mason-Dixon line and announced all the black performers had to sit in the back. We were naive, just a bunch of kids. There wasn't anything to do but take it. We were booked at these places and we were expected to perform.

We played at places that looked more like barns than theaters. We'd follow a rodeo or whatever. There was a rope down the middle. Black folks on one side, whites on the other, although sometimes there was mingling when the music got going.

The white acts would stay at the better hotels. We'd get shuttled out to some rooming house on the outskirts of town. Then the next day, we'd all get back in the bus and move on.

We had trouble even in the North. I have a fair complexion and some people can't distinguish my racial background. I booked the group some rooms at this hotel in Detroit. When the rest of the guys showed up, the guy behind the desk took one look and said he must have made a mistake, that there weren't any rooms after all. You got used to it. You did what you were supposed to do and then you left.

It was a good time. What we did was once called race music. We've come a long way from that and I'm proud of the part our group played. My only regret is that we didn't come 10 years later. We'd all be millionaires.

BERMAN PATTERSON sang lead tenor for the Cleftones, a doo-wop quintet from Queens, New York. They charted with "Little Girl of Mine" and "Heart and Soul." He retired from the New York Department of Corrections and works for the Department of Children and Families in Florida.

THE CLEFTONES

little girl of mine

vehicle

A lot of people said we sounded like Blood, Sweat and Tears. I'd have to admit that it's hard to listen to our "Vehicle" and say we're all that different. But the truth is we tried to give them the song. Jim [Peterik, lead singer] went backstage after one of their shows and tried to get them to listen to a cassette of it. They pooh-poohed him like he was some kid from the audience.

Some members of Blood, Sweat and Tears saw us after "Vehicle" came out. They recognized Jim and said they had been kicking themselves in the butt. We were strongly influenced by their music, but we weren't copying them.

Before "Vehicle" came out in 1970, we did "You Wouldn't Listen to Me" on Parrot, the same record label that Tom Jones and Engelbert Humperdinck were on. We later did "L.A. Goodbye" that got to No. 7 on the charts. After that, we never got back in the top 40.

We still perform in the spring and summer. There are seven of us on stage and six are from the original Ides of March that formed when we were in high school. We just stayed together. I look at us as I would a bowling team. It's still a fun thing to do.

LARRY MILLAS played guitar and bass for the Ides of March. He's a recording engineer and producer in Chicago.

a wonderful dream

I drive a bus for an elementary school. The children know about my records, but if I played our songs for them, I'm sure it would put them to sleep. It's all that hip-hop stuff now.

Back in the '50s, it seemed like every neighborhood in Philadelphia had its own doo-wop group. It was just like you see it portrayed in the movies. We'd rehearse on street corners or maybe go to the subway to get that echo-chamber effect. When we got older, we sang in bars and developed a good following. The military interrupted us for a few years, but we got back together in the early '60s.

We were five guys who simply loved to sing. It didn't matter how much we were paid. They'd offer us $25 apiece for an entire weekend and we'd say sure.

After "Wonderful Dream," we got involved with an agent in South Carolina and played some one-nighters in the South. Most times, we were able to avoid the racism, but I remember this one day near Stone Mountain, Georgia, when we were driving to our next engagement. The traffic slowed to a crawl and we asked somebody what the problem was. He told us there was a KKK rally up ahead. That made our hearts beat faster, I'll tell you that.

FRANK TROUTT sang with the Majors. The Philadelphia-based group charted with "A Wonderful Dream" in 1962.

beep-beep

We were all in the same fraternity at the University of Connecticut. We were musicians at first—I was the drummer— and then we evolved into singing and then comedy. After college, we worked a lot of lounges where the people expected to be entertained. You couldn't just give them one tune after another.

We had a very unique style. Groups like the Four Preps and the Lettermen looked up to us.

These days I'm a humorous speaker at dinners and meetings. They'll introduce me as a professor, and people will think it's going to be just another boring presentation. Then I'll sing "Beep-Beep" or another one of our songs and it always goes over well.

We wrote that song based on a night when the Playmates were going to an engagement. We were driving a Cadillac and this little Nash Rambler kept trying to pass us. We were going back and forth, changing lanes and stuff. Toying with the guy like that gave us the idea.

DONNY CONN was a member of the Playmates. In 1958 he and Chic Hetti penned "Beep Beep," their top-charting song.

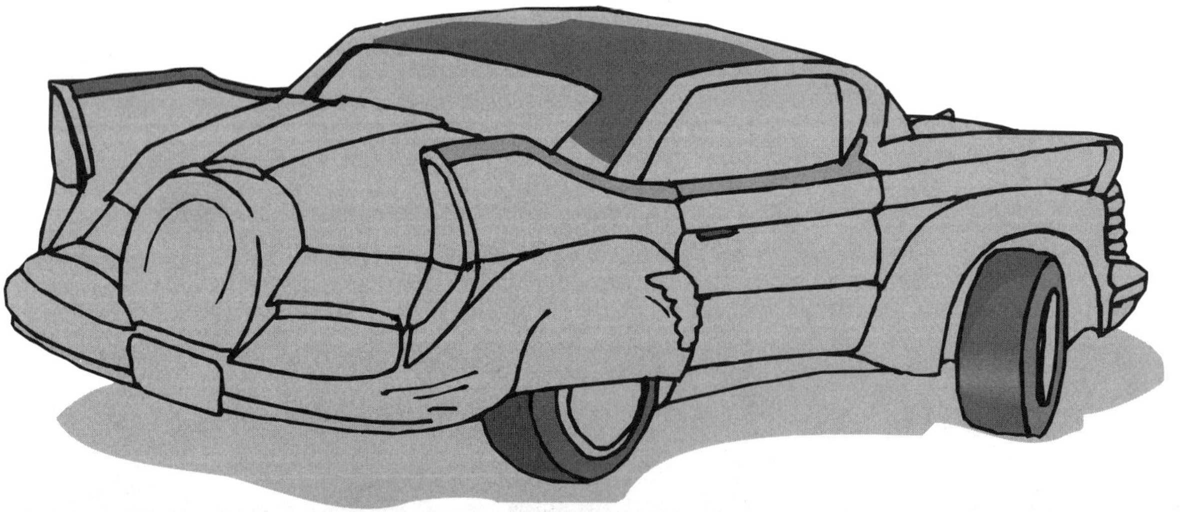

THE PLAYMATES

1910 FRUITGUM COMPANY

For us, it was a matter of being at the right place at the right time. We were a high school band from Linden, New Jersey, playing at places like swim clubs. The father of one of the group members happened to strike up a conversation with record producers Jerry Kasenetz and Jeff Katz. "Simon Says" had already been recorded by a Philadelphia group, but they didn't like that version and wanted to find out if we could do it better.

The other guys in the band weren't excited about that because they considered the tune too trivial. They were 17 and 18, so I was the voice of wisdom at 21. I said, hey, let's do what they say and ride it out, and later we can do the music we want.

I was the one who suggested the "Wooly Bully"-type sound for the background. They took my advice and that was the arrangement that made the final cut.

But the guys were still saying the songs we were doing weren't serious enough, and by the fall of 1968 there were only two original members left. We hadn't seen any money in all this time and I asked them to pay up. That didn't work, so we filed suit. That's when Jeff and Jerry threw me out. We ended up settling for something like 40 grand. That's not a whole lot for two gold records.

People used to make fun of us for being a bubblegum group. That might have been the label that was put on us, but we were really a very good hard-rock band. We went on one night in Minneapolis when Vanilla Fudge cancelled out and we had the crowd roaring. I don't feel that we compromised ourselves. I was excited with the amount of commercial success we had.

FRANK JECKELL played guitar for the 1910 Fruitgum Company that gave us "Simon Says" and "1, 2, 3 Red Light" in 1968. These days, he installs computer programs for IBM.

simon says

walk on by

I got initiated into the facts of life early in my career when a disc jockey in Chicago wound up with his name as co-writer of my first million-seller, "Auctioneer." I had written the song in its entirety two years before I even knew he existed. In today's money, he probably cheated me out of at least a half million dollars.

We looked around for a follow-up to "Walk on By" and thought we had something with "If a Woman Answers, Hang Up the Phone," but a bunch of women from Chicago got together and decided it was advocating immoral behavior. It eventually got banned. You couldn't fight that kind of thing back then. It still sold half a million copies, though, and that wasn't bad.

People are always sending me songs. I've got a truckload. Cassettes, reel-to-reel—whatever. I never throw anything away, and I always listen to material sent to me. You never know what's going to happen.

Kendall Hayes wrote "Walk on By," and he died a few years ago. I'm standing there in the viewing room six feet from the casket and this guy comes up and pitches me a song on cassette right in the middle of the funeral home. I took it, because I didn't want to cause a scene. There's one thing I know for sure; there are some people out there who have no taste.

LEROY VAN DYKE, formerly a reporter and an auctioneer, recorded "Walk on By" in 1961. It stayed on the country charts for 42 weeks (19 weeks at No. 1) and got up to No. 2 on the pop meter. He continues in all types of shows in the United States, Canada and overseas.

LEROY VAN DYKE

SOUL SURVIVORS

We were doing a lot of work as backup singers when [record producers] Kenny Gamble and Leon Huff heard us and started a beautiful relationship. You have to understand the racial thing back then. There was quite a separation as to what was black music and what was white music. Kenny and Leon worked with the O'Jays and the Spinners and all those other wonderful black groups of Philadelphia. We were the only white group they had any success with.

People always said the Soul Survivors sounded black. We didn't think that we sounded like anything. People were mistaking sincerity and heartfelt musical expression for soul. But having said that, we worked a lot of black clubs and when the promoters saw us, lots of times their mouths would drop.

I remember when we played the Paramount Theater in Newark during the height of the race riots. We were literally held hostage inside the building because of all the stuff going on in the streets. Given the tension, we were advised not to perform. But we were an ornery bunch. Sometimes we didn't know if we were in a band or a gang. We didn't come there to punk out. Jackie Wilson finished his set and people started to leave. It wasn't a good vibe at all. We got out there and immediately started playing "Expressway." It was amazing. Just the one song could turn an audience completely around. They were clapping and dancing. I'm only 18, 19 years old, but I knew I was in the middle of almost a religious experience. It was blessed magic and one of our best performances.

RICHARD INGUI performed with the Soul Survivors. The group had a major hit with "Expressway to Your Heart" in 1967 and continues to tour.

expressway to your heart

wipe-out

We formed the band in 1962 when I was a freshman in high school. We came up with a thing called "Surfer Joe" and each guy kicked in 20 bucks so we could get it recorded. The idea was to press 100 copies to sell at school so we could buy a guitar amp.

We couldn't figure out what to put on the other side of the record. We did this pathetic version of "Peter Gunn" and that was a no-go. Then we tried an instrumental version of "Heartbreak Hotel." Nothing. Then something called "Hot Dogging." Still nothing. Then we decided to just let Ronnie [Wilson] play the drums. Our manager had this wild cackle like Goofy from the cartoons, so that's how "Wipe-Out" started. We added a sound that was like somebody falling off a surfboard and spliced it on the tape. It went on from there with a great deal of wound-up energy that was the band's trademark.

There were a lot of lawsuits in the years that followed. My parents ended up selling my share of "Wipe-Out" for $3,200.

We still perform occasionally, although certainly not enough to make a living. One thing we like to do is get people to come on stage and try to play the drums for "Wipe-Out." It's been more than 35 years, but the song remains incredibly popular. Half the autographs we give are to kids under 21.

JIM PASH played the sax and cornet for the Surfaris. These days, he repairs instruments and teaches at a music school. The group's 'Wipe-Out" was one of the biggest hits of 1963.

THE SURFARIS

green-eyed lady

The key for us was getting hooked up with producer Frank Slay, who worked with Strawberry Alarm Clock. We all thought it would go on forever, that we were invincible or something, but we only lasted about three years.

I later became the road manager for War and Tanya Tucker, but I stopped doing that in 1980. Every time I'd go to California the people I knew there were either divorced, addicted or in rehab. I didn't want that kind of life so I settled in Arkansas. I was in the fast-food business for a while, but that was like working in the emergency room. I ran a bowling center and then I followed my hobby and got into landscaping. I get out and do people's lawns. I love it.

I have no desire to get back into music. Once you've done it at a certain level, you don't want to step back just to be near it in a half-assed way.

BOB MACVITTIE was the drummer for Sugarloaf, a rock quartet from Denver that had a hit with "Green-Eyed Lady" in 1970.

RICHARD GOTTEHRER

We wrote "Boyfriend" at the piano the way we did all our songs. Bob had been in a candy store in Brooklyn when he overheard a conversation between some teenage girls. One was talking in a little bit of a threatening way, and the other was saying things like, well, wait until my boyfriend gets here and he'll beat the shit out of you, or something like that. Bob brought that back to us and we worked it into a tune.

We not only wrote the song and produced it, but we placed it on the record label. That was a very important development, because writer-producers weren't doing that type of thing. It was a step toward becoming independent producers.

RICHARD GOTTEHRER was a member of the songwriting team (along with Jerry Goldstein and Bob Feldman) that composed "My Boyfriend's Back" for the Angels. The trio also performed as the Strangeloves in the mid 1960s. Today , Gottehrer works with a company that distributes original music to record companies via the Internet.

my boyfriend's back

feeling groovy

In the early 1960s, we were four kids from the little town of Santa Cruz, California, saving our money to go to the big city, San Francisco, and make hit records. About every six months, we'd cut five new songs, all originals, at a small studio in the city, and then begin the trek south to Hollywood to pitch the record companies.

On our third trip to L.A., we thought we'd hit it when we auditioned for Nick Venet, whose claim to fame (at the time, it was a major one) was that he produced the Beach Boys. This was pre-Brian Wilson. He said, literally, "I'm going to make you stars." After six months of waiting, we never heard from him again.

We gave up on L.A. and decided to hound a small label in San Francisco owned by two DJs, Tom Donahue and Bob Mitchell, who had come from Philadelphia to start a company called Autumn Records. They had signed a local group, the Beau Brummels, and given that they were doing back-to-back shows on San Francisco's biggest rock station, KYA, they would play the Brummels' first record, "Laugh, Laugh" incessantly, forcing it into becoming a hit.

We pitched tapes to Donahue and Mitchell for almost a year before they finally signed us. No sooner had the ink dried on our contract than we learned they were bankrupt. Fortunately, they sold the entire Autumn roster (which included the Mojo

Men, the Beau Brummels and Sly Stewart, later Sly and the Family Stone) to Warner Brothers.

Warners assigned a rookie producer to us by the name of Lenny Waronker, whose father, Si, had just sold his own label (which produced David Seville and the Chipmunks). Having some clout in Hollywood, Si got his son a job at Warner's. Lenny had never produced a thing, but when he heard our demos, he suggested that we cover a tune from the as-yet-unreleased Simon and Garfunkel album along with some songs by an unknown songwriter friend of his named Randy Newman. We loved Randy's stuff, but hated the Paul Simon tune. Even so, Warners went with it and thus, "Feeling Groovy" was born.

Many years later, I learned that the only reason Donahue and Mitchell signed us was to stop our constant door-pounding. They never thought we had any talent.

DICK SCOPPETTONE (second from right) played guitar for the pop-rock group Harper's Bizarre. These days, he's a travel agent and a writer.

HARPER'S BIZARRE

life is but a dream

I knew Alan Freed pretty well. He did a lot for the music, I will say that, but I found him a very arrogant man who thought he was God. He also had the bad habit of putting his name on songs, but fortunately that never happened with us.

I played the piano for the Harptones and didn't do as much singing as the other five guys. What some people don't know is that I also had a female group by the name of the Joy Tones. I'd do a show with the Harptones and then come right back and work with the girls.

I'm 72 years old and that's a long time to be in music. The Harptones hit a bad time in the mid-'60s and we split up. The group got back together in 1972 and we still do a couple of shows a month.

I've got a recording studio at my home and I can generate my own CDs over the Internet. It's two girls and myself. It's really a fun thing.

RAOUL CITA (lower right at right, lower left below) formed the Harptones in 1953. Their "Life Is But a Dream" reached No. 3 on the rhythm-and-blues charts in 1955.

THE HARPTONES

JOHNNY AND THE HURRICANES

red river rock

I got burned out on the music business. How would you like to ride in an old bus for 300 miles night after night after night to the next show? It was called the Dick Clark Road Show and we traveled with artists like Paul Anka and Freddy Cannon. When you live with guys 24 hours a day, there's going to be a lot of animosity within the group. Plus the fact that the rest of the Hurricanes were from Toledo [Ohio] and I was from Detroit.

The last I heard from the band was about 15 years ago. They wanted to get back together for some bookings in Sweden. I said how much and they said $500 plus expenses. I told them to forget it.

The Hurricanes were on *American Bandstand* six times, but getting the money was another story. I thought all the bills were getting paid, but it didn't happen. Three years after I left the group, the tax man came and said I owed thousands. I didn't have enough left for toothpaste. That'll tend to sour you on the music industry.

It's been 40 years, but I still get the fan letters. To tell the truth, I'm reluctant to answer them. There were a lot of girls back then and, well, you know. But I got to travel and see this beautiful country and meet some wonderful people.

BO SAVICH was the drummer for Johnny and the Hurricanes. The instrumental band had a hit with "Red River Rock" in 1959.

green tambourine

In 1961, I got some mates together and formed Ivan and the Sabers. I wrote a song called "Just Let Her Go" that was enough of a hit to enable us to open for the big names that came through Ohio. This was in 1964 and the Rolling Stones were making their first American tour. Only 700 people showed up in Dayton, Ohio, in a hall that seated 5,000 and the promoter lost money and almost came to blows with Mick.

We backed up Jan and Dean at the Coconut Lounge in Springfield, Ohio. They were touring alone and depending on the promoter to provide backup bands at each city. We were in the audience one night waiting for them to come on. There was some delay and I went backstage to see what the problem was. The local band must have chickened out because they claimed their sheet music blew out the window. Naturally, Ivan and the Sabers saved the day. We jumped out of the audience and backed up Jan and Dean. After the show, Dean reached into his jeans pocket and pulled out a wad of bills, but we were so blown out by getting to do such a cool thing that we declined the money.

I quit the Sabers and transferred from the University of Cincinnati to the Miami University in Oxford, Ohio, where I replaced Tony of Tony and the Bandits. We changed the name to the Lemon Pipers. (I hated that stupid name.)

We opened for groups like the Jefferson Airplane and the Lovin' Spoonful. It wasn't long after we opened for John Sebastian that we signed with his record label, Kama Sutra. I think he was impressed by my rendition of "Louie, Louie" sung as "Mrs. Miller" from the Merv Griffin Show.

By September of 1968 my monthly pay was $25. I quit the Lemon Pipers, went back to college, graduated in 1969 and moved to San Francisco. We went from college bar band to No. 1 and back to a college bar band in less than a year.

IVAN BROWNE (center) was the lead singer for the Lemon Pipers, the one-hit wonders who gave us "Green Tambourine" in 1968. Today he lives in Mendocino County, California, on 10 acres bought from Ray Manzarek's (Doors) family. He performs with his wife in the Ivan and Isa Band.

★ STAR PERFORMER—Sides registering greatest proportionate

THIS WEEK	1 Wk. Ago	2 Wks. Ago	3 Wks. Ago	TITLE Artist (Producer), Label & Number	Weeks On Chart
Billboard Award	3	5	9	GREEN TAMBOURINE Lemon Pipers (Paul Leka), Buddah 23	8
2	1	1	2	JUDY IN DISGUISE (With Glasses) John Fred & His Playboy Band (J. Fred & A. Bernard), Paula 282	11
3	2	2	6	CHAIN OF FOOLS Aretha Franklin (Jerry Wexler), Atlantic 2464	9
★ 4	7	16	23	SPOOKY Classics IV (Buddy Buie), Imperial 66259	7
5	5	7	7	BEND ME, SHAPE ME American Breed (Bill Traut), Acta 811	10
6	4	4	4	WOMAN, WOMAN Union Gap (Jerry Fuller), Columbia 44297	12
★ 7	18	47	84	LOVE IS BLUE Paul Mauriat, Philips 40495	5

LEMON PIPERS

the enchanted sea

In 1956, I was doing some work for Dave Brubeck. I was single and tired and decided to go on a cruise. I just wanted to get away from music for a while. One of the people in my cabin was a dentist named Warren Nadel who was also a songwriter. We became friends and started working on songs together.

We came up with this piece that sounded like water. I'm from Germany, so I wasn't as good with language as Warren was. He came up with the title, "Enchanted Sea." I played the accordion and the piano and he did the guitar. We added some sound effects and, to our surprise, we had a hit record.

To be candid, I would not consider that song as my best work. But I was a young man, and I guess it was all right for the time.

FRANK METIS was a member of the Islanders that charted with "The Enchanted Sea" in 1959. Now an arranger, he has written 150 piano books.

The Association had its roots when a 13-piece folk/rock band that called themselves The Men went defunct. I was auditioning at the Ice House in Pasadena when I was accepted into the new group. We didn't perform at all for the first six months. Our manager gave us $5 a day and a place to stay, which turned out to be an old house that was also our rehearsal hall. For spending money, we did demo sessions for other rock groups. We took a great deal of time to polish our sound until we had what we wanted.

I never heard of any radio stations that banned "Along Came Mary" because of alleged drug references, but there was this instance when we were booked to play on graduation night at Disney. The guard knew we were the group that recorded "Mary" and he wasn't going to let us into the park.

We showed him a clipping from some Catholic girls' school that had "Mary" in it—I forget the name—that quoted the girls as saying the tune was their theme song. The guy read it and said we could come in.

We've had an amazing run when you think of it. There was no way to possibly imagine back in 1967 that people would still want to hear "Windy" more than three decades later. The band has never stopped touring with at least two original members. Nobody has a problem with my singing Association songs with the Preps. We had a very amicable parting of the ways. That's a rarity these days and I'm very glad for it.

JIM YESTER was an original member of the Association, a Los Angeles-based band that had major hits with "Along Came Mary," "Windy" and "Cherish." He continues to perform with the Preps, an oldies group featuring Bruce Belland of the original Four Preps and David Somerville of the Diamonds.

along came mary

pipeline

We were all in Santa Ana (California) High School together. Brian (Carman, also a guitarist) and I had an idea for a melody and we put the pieces together after school. First, we called it "Liberty's Whip" and then we thought ".44 Magnum" sounded cool. Nothing clicked until one day when Warren Waters, our bass player, and I went to a surfing movie and heard the reference to "Bonzai Pipeline." That's when we had our title.

We didn't get the big head when the tune became a hit. It may have been that we were so young that it didn't register. We continued to play local dances and assemblies just like we had been doing. We went on tour that summer, but we continued going to school.

There was a definite slow-up when the Beatles and Rolling Stones came out. We started covering their songs just to maintain a rapport with the audience. The funny thing was, there were several other good singles we came up with after "Pipeline." The record company wanted to wait until that song went completely off the chart before pushing another tune. In my opinion, they waited too long and the moment was lost.

People always ask if we surfed or if we just sang about it. Well, we really surfed. I live just a short distance from the beach. I might be a grandfather, but I go out every chance I get.

BOB SPICKARD (second from right at right, second from left in top row above above) plays lead guitar for the surf group, the Chantays. Their "Pipeline" was a big hit in 1963. Spickard still performs with the group and also has an industrial equipment company.

THE CHANTAYS

can't you hear my heartbeat?

I'm totally unhip. Like for example, I've always been interested in trains. When I came to America, one of the first places I went was Altoona in Pennsylvania. People thought I went there looking for girls. Actually, I heard the town had a real neat train station and I wanted to see it.

I knew Jim Morrison (of the Doors), but I've always found people who do drugs boring. All the men get in a room by themselves trying to find the meaning of life, or whatever it is they're looking for. Their girlfriends are in the other room. That's where you'd find me.

We were always billed as the dichotomy to the Rolling Stones. I never had any trouble with our image because it wasn't an act. It was the way we were. I've always thought it would be so exhausting to be Mick Jagger. He's an extremely intelligent man and a good person to be around. But on cue he has to pretend to be a Cockney snob who hates everything and everybody. Just to keep up that image.

I was very influenced by the Beatles. When I was 16, I ran with them quite a bit and we constantly talked about music. Nowadays, rock stars talk about their hair when they get together. That is, if they get together at all. There's so much jealousy. Paul was my mentor. I remember being in his limousine one day and we stopped at a drug store. Paul walked in and asked for toothpaste. The woman behind the counter recognized him and got very excited. Paul was chatty and friendly the whole time. I walked out of there realizing there's something to being nice to people.

When I was 13, I knew the names of almost all the people in the bands. I don't think young people today care. They simply don't identify with the musicians. And the groups don't stay together these days either. It's like they go on tour, stare at each other, say "I hate you" and then it's over. By contrast, we were working-class people. We might not love the people we hung around with, but we did what it took to make it work.

Back then, rock groups shared song information with each other. That's completely gone. It's like they put it all in a vault. And we shared ourselves, too. Jimmy Page and John Paul Jones (of Led Zeppelin) played on some of my albums. And I'm on some of Dave Clark's records. I stomp my feet. I was very good at that.

PETER NOONE was the lead singer for Herman's Hermits of "Can't You Hear My Heartbeat?" fame. He continues to tour with a fresh batch of Hermits.

HERMAN'S HERMITS

classical gas

I wrote the song after a wild two-week gig in Las Vegas with the Smothers Brothers. I think we must have stayed awake for the entire two weeks. I don't think I took my shades off the whole time, except maybe to wash my face. When we finally left, I went home, slept for a couple of days, got up and spent the weekend alone with the guitar. I had, for the most part, been concentrating on writing comedy for *The Smothers Brothers Show*, and had not touched the guitar for quite a while, but that weekend I enjoyed getting back into it and worked out the basic idea for the piece.

I didn't really have any big plans for it, other than maybe to have a piece to play at parties when they passed the guitar around. I thought of it simply as repertoire or fuel for the classical guitar, so I called it "Classical Gasoline."

During the second season of the *Comedy Hour,* I worked on the piece off and on for a couple of months. I began to record *The Mason Williams Phonograph Record* that fall and "Classical Gasoline" was one of the tunes to be included. On the parts for the session, the music copyist inadvertently abbreviated "Gasoline" to "Gas," so that's how it actually got its title.

The song still receives a fair amount of airplay, and I am delighted that it has become somewhat of a utilitarian piece of music for people to use for their own creations.

MASON WILLIAMS composed the well-known instrumental, "Classical Gas," in 1967. It went to No. 1 and won three Grammy awards.

MASON WILLIAMS

tears on my pillow

We got through doing "Cha-Cha Henry" at a recording session and somebody said, hey, that didn't sound like too much, why don't you try the other tune on the demo? We had only heard "Tears" a couple of times and weren't that familiar with it, but we did it in our doo-wop style. Everybody stopped what they were doing and told us to record it on the spot. And that's what we did. You could do loosey-goosey things like that back then.

Technology has changed the music business. Now you've got drum machines and everything else that's moved the sound from the manual to the electronic. We need to find a happy medium. It's allowed people without a great deal of talent to perform a song. When we were coming up, you had to have talent or you didn't go anywhere.

One of the things that has always helped the Imperials is that we exposed ourselves to different kinds of music. We went to Carnegie Hall. We listened to Sammy Davis, Jr., and Frank Sinatra and Ella Fitzgerald. We were a lot more open-minded than some of the other groups.

My favorite song is "Hurts So Bad." There are some tunes that you relate to vocally or personally or a combination of the two. That's definitely it for me. I always sing it in a very heartfelt way because it reaches the deepest part of my soul. I was always one of those people who was in love with love. We were very fortunate to work on that project with Don Costa. He arranged for Sinatra and his stylings stimulated us very much.

ANTHONY GOURDINE (top) is the name behind Little Anthony and the Imperials. The Brooklyn rhythm-and-blues band had hits with "Tears On My Pillow" in 1958 and "Hurt So Bad" seven years later. The group continues to perform.

LITTLE ANTHONY & THE IMPERIALS

yummy, yummy, yummy

I started at 15 and was with the band about four years. Dale Powers and I were dissatisfied with the music and agreed to join another band managed by Pat Bennett, singer Tony's wife. We even moved to her residence to practice, but we never released anything because Dale got drafted and I joined the Air Force National Guard.

When I look back on the Ohio Express, the word "manipulated" definitely comes to mind. Jerry Kasenetz and Jeff Katz had an idea for a sound and we were selected to promote their material. But the misconception people have is that we were put together specifically for that purpose when, in fact, we were already a working band. We had no control whatsoever of the money or anything else. The contract called for us to release X number of singles and albums per year and that's what we did. We did the bubblegum thing like we were told, but a few of our compositions made the B sides.

The travel part of it was ridiculous. We'd be in Cleveland one day and Los Angeles the next. Once we were in New Orleans and missed our plane to Cleveland. That plane crashed. It's like we were always on the run and nobody knew exactly where or why.

At that time we made around $2,000 per show, which was pretty good money. Some of that was supposed to go into a trust fund, but I've never seen it. I'm not bitter financially, though. I'm a born-again Christian with a wonderful family and I feel I've been blessed by God. For me to have bad thoughts would be putting myself in chains.

Did we like the bubblegum music we were playing? Not really. We were into Cream and Hendrix and that's what we played a lot at our concerts. Jerry and Jeff never said anything about that kind of mix. I guess it was all right with them as long as it didn't get on a record.

DEAN KASTRAN played bass with the Ohio Express, the bubblegum band that had hits with "Yummy, Yummy, Yummy" and "Chewy, Chewy" in the late 1960s These days, he works in sales and occasionally sings in a duet.

KAY STARR

When RCA offered me "Waltz," I thought they had made a big mistake. My voice was bluesy and blood-and-guts and here they were wanting me to sing a Jack-and-Jill-went-up-the-hill song. I tried to get them to give it to someone else on the record label.

But they kept telling me it would work, that the song was more than just a Mom and Dad rocking in their living room. I finally said, OK, I'll do it, but I want the Dramamine concession.

I went to Ireland on vacation. The record people called and told me I'd have to come back. I said whatever for. Then they told me the damn record was a hit and I'd have to do promotional work for it. The song stayed on top for six weeks. I didn't think I could do a merry sunshine song, but I guess I was wrong.

KAY STARR had a No. 1 hit in 1956 with "Rock and Roll Waltz." In the 1940s, she sang with several Big Band groups including Glenn Miller. She continues to perform.

RAY CONNIFF

somewhere my love

In those days [the sixties], radio stations were either country or pop. There wasn't any crossover. Marty Robbins had a country hit with "Singing the Blues," and Mitch Miller wanted me to record it with Guy Mitchell. Marty did OK with his version, but Guy got way up in the pop charts with his cover. Marty called Mitch and said, "What the hell are you doing taking my song and clobbering it?"

Mitch told Marty he'd make it up to him. We did "White Sport Coat" together and it was a nice-sized hit. I had never met Marty before the recording session. For most musicians, the first thing they want to know is, "What's the tempo?" Marty came prancing up and asked, "What's the speed?"

What music did I listen to on my home stereo back then? To tell the truth, I didn't have the time. When I was assigned a project, I worked as hard as I could to make it a hit record. I was doing two or three albums a year plus playing trombone on radio stations. There wasn't time to do single backings.

"Somewhere My Love" competed with the Beatles and Rolling Stones and all those other pop tunes. It was fun following it up the charts. The song almost didn't get recorded, though. The publisher showed it around, but nobody wanted to do it. I went with it and it was by far the biggest thing I've ever done.

RAY CONNIFF played trombone during the Big Band era. He was the arranger/conductor for Columbia Records' top vocalists in the 1950s and '60s. His "Somewhere My Love" from the movie *Dr. Zhivago* was a big hit in 1966.

kisses sweeter than wine

I don't think what we did was all that political. People just made it that way. We were just singing our songs. We sang for anybody who would listen and, as it turned out, a lot of that audience was left-wing groups.

In some ways getting blacklisted was good because it got us out of the nightclubs and into the concert halls, which was more fun. We never got an official apology from anybody. Hey, Ronald Reagan said there wasn't a blacklist.

We got "Kisses Sweeter Than Wine" in a roundabout way. Leadbelly used to sing the tune, which was an old Irish song about a dead cow. Pete heard him singing and thought it sounded right for us. Lee Hays wrote some lyrics and the rest of us stuck our two cents in.

The Weavers was a happy time for me and definitely the most important musical period of my life.

FRED HELLERMAN (far right at left, center above) performed with the Weavers, a folk group that featured Pete Seeger. Their hits in the mid-1950s included "Kisses Sweeter Than Wine." They were blacklisted in the communist witch hunt of the '50s, but later their chief accuser admitted he fabricated the whole thing. Hellerman occasionally writes music for TV and movies.

at the hop

We were lucky. You had to be. You had to have the right song, the right studio, the right label and the right promotion. Dick Clark was just starting out with *American Bandstand* when we came out. He heard us play "Do the Bop" and suggested we change the title. He said the bop is going to be history by the time we press the record and we'll miss the boat. But he said there will always be hops. So we changed the line and it worked big. Like I said, we were lucky.

They wanted a fast follow-up to that song and that's where "Rock and Roll Is Here to Stay" comes in. The newspapers were giving pop music a hard time, saying it wasn't any good and it wasn't going to last. My dad heard that line on the B side of a Little Richard tune and said, hey, why don't you guys wrap a tune around it and come out with it as a kind of protest song? He said it would be our way of striking back. Dad was a club fighter with Angelo Dundee, so he was used to striking back. We took his advice and it worked. Lucky again.

JOE TERRY sang with Danny and the Juniors, a Philadelphia-based quartet that had a No. 1 hit in 1958 with "At the Hop." Their "Rock and Roll Is Here to Stay," released the same year, made the top 20. The group continues to perform.

DANNY & THE JUNIORS

slow walk

I had just signed with Mercury Records and was appearing in Wildwood, New Jersey. It was a Sunday night. The man from Mercury came to the club and asked if I could come to New York City the next day to make a record. I told him I would make it my business to be there. I wrote the whole night long to prepare for the session, and that's when "Slow Walk" popped up. I got the outline in my head and did the charts when we got to the studio. Things moved quickly back then. We did three takes and that was it. I didn't hear much about the record until I got the word from Cashbox that we had a No. 3 record.

Studio musicians in New York back then got $86 a session. If you were the leader, you got double. I received that plus the record deal. I worked hard for the 12 years I was at Mercury. If I wasn't doing folk, I was doing country and western. My band only lasted for seven years after 1956. It took more time than I had. Since then I've been freelancing.

It's hard to look back on that period of time without thinking about the money. I lost millions. All the artists did. There was just no way to keep up with it. I've gotten some of it back, though. They say the squeaky wheel gets the grease. Well, I'm the squeaky wheel. I'm doing the best of my ability to keep the crooks out of my money.

Tenor saxophonist SIL AUSTIN charted with "Slow Walk" in 1956. He has recorded more than 30 albums ranging from performances with the New York Philharmonic to the Ray Charles Singers. He continues to play all over the world.

SIL AUSTIN

rock and roll is here to stay

I was 18, the youngest performer at Woodstock. There were 12 of us in the group at that time and we got $300 for appearing. The check bounced. We were given a dollar for appearing in the documentary about the festival. Come to think of it, I don't remember getting that either. We never were too concerned about that because the exposure we received was tremendous. We were a bunch of guys from Columbia University playing our eighth gig, and here we were with Crosby, Stills and Nash.

The bass player and I drove to the festival in a beat-up VW van. We got there on a Friday and just camped out while we were waiting to play. We got bumped the entire weekend and didn't go on until the sun came up Monday morning and the place looked like a refugee camp. They had a pavilion set up for performers, but there was such a need for health care that they took it over for emergency cases. We were all one — the acts and the crowd.

Looking back, it was really a scary scene. The stage was sinking in the mud. Literally. The people who put the show together were teetering on disaster.

My mood about being at Woodstock went back and forth. Listening to the music, there was no place I'd rather be. But the rain and the mud and the not sleeping because we didn't know when we were going on — that stuff got old.

JOHN "JOCKO" MARCELLINO is the drummer for Sha Na Na, a 1950s revival band that appeared at Woodstock. He has stayed with the group since its inception in 1969.

SHA NA NA

denise

When we started out, we called ourselves Junior and the Counts. The record company didn't like that, so they changed us to Randy and the Rainbows. Never mind that there wasn't anybody named Randy in the group. We were only 16 and 17 years old, so we didn't have a lot of say in the matter.

We auditioned for the Tokens. They liked the way we sang "Denise" so they agreed to produce us. The follow-up to that was "Why Do Kids Grow Up?" and it was just getting started when President Kennedy was assassinated. That put a damper on the whole music business. Then we did a great song called "Happy Teenager," but it didn't get much airplay because that's when the Beatles came. After that, only the big groups could survive and we faded from the scene.

I had my own card and gift shop for a while, but that folded and now I'm a fire-sprinkler inspector. The band still plays occasionally at weddings and at celebrity functions for people like Fabian.

Mike Zero (second from left at right, bottom right below) played with Randy and the Rainbows, a doo-wop group from Queens, New York. Their biggest hit was "Denise" in 1963.

RANDY & THE RAINBOWS

tequila

I started my own band in 1952 and three years later I went to work for Bill Randle, a big boy in the DJ circle. In his line of work, he was in a position to get records early. If he heard something good, he'd have me make an arrangement of it.

That's what happened with "Tequila." The Champs' version was doing well on the West Coast. Bill told me to leave nothing out, but it was all right if I wanted to add to it. So I wrote the sax solo in the middle and did some things with the harmonies.

The kids Bill picked to play the record tried hard, but they were slow at picking up new arrangements. I got some of my guys to come to the session and we cut the record in a half hour.

Bill had the song that night on his radio show. I thought that was a big mistake. The Champs were still on the charts and we'd get confused with them. But he did it anyway.

They sold about about 700,000 copies of theirs and we did about 300,000 with ours. It was very unusual for two groups to have the same song at about the same time, but those were the early days of pop and those things happened.

EDDIE PLATT, a saxophonist/bandleader from Cleveland, arranged a second version of the hit single "Tequila" in 1958.

My involvement lasted about three years. John Lennon got involved with the band in 1972, but I was out of it by then.

I played mostly with big bands and worked with Woody Herman among many others. Then I looked around for a rock band that was already established to add our horns to. Elephant happened at about the same time Blood, Sweat and Tears and Chicago did.

Our managers wanted us to be the next Beatles, so they came up with the idea for crazy costumes and wild stage shows. We'd perform in leotards and had this jungle of a stage where plastic animals blew up while we were playing. My old lady designed my silver belt and my silver Army boots. Then I put a wreath on top of my head. It was really stupid.

Bikers started hanging around with the band. Everybody was into different drugs. Wine, coke, speed, pot — everybody's head was in a different place. I became unhappy with the scene. Plus we weren't doing very many gigs. I ended up leaving to go to work for Tommy James without the Shondells.

MYRON YULES was a horn player for Elephant's Memory. Some of their music appeared on the soundtrack of the film, "Midnight Cowboy." Their biggest hit was "Mongoose" in 1970.

mongoose

my girl josephine

"Josephine" was written by Fats Domino back in the 1950s. I had always played the song at dances because it got such a good response. We put it out on the B side, but that's the one the people liked. You never know in the music business.

I'm satisfied with my career. I hit it hard for 10 years and then I just got tired of the road. Things changed and my kind of music switched over to country. You were considered an outsider unless you lived in Nashville. So I got in the nightclub and lounge business and that turned out OK.

I still play here and there but do a lot of fishing in between. Rockabilly kinda died in the United States, but it's big in Sweden. I went in 1995 and again in 1999 and the crowds were very enthusiastic.

Arkansas-born JERRY JAYE had a hit with "My Girl Josephine" in 1967.

JERRY JAYE

diddy wah diddy

The group was definitely a trailblazer. The music was created to be sound sculpture. The way it's layered you're reminded more of Van Gogh and Picasso than something coming from a record.

To say that Don [Van Vliet, aka Captain Beefheart] was dictatorial was putting it mildly. He literally tried to brainwash us during the 12-hour recording sessions. There was sleep deprivation. There was food deprivation. No drugs, though. Don was a brilliant musician, but he had no people skills other than to manipulate. He kept us on that killer schedule for a year. Finally, I said to myself, why am I putting up with this shit? This is stupid. I'm leaving. There was one other thing to consider as well. No paydays. Other than the per diems while I was on the road, I played for free.

Everybody in the group had another name. Mine was Zoot Horn Rollo. The idea was that we were doing things from another planet. We were living inside an art school.

I settled down and became normal. I've done some teaching and I've managed a retail music store. Lately, I've been doing some recording with local people around Eugene, Oregon. No pressure like before. Just fun.

BILL HARKLEROAD played guitar for Captain Beefheart and the Magic Band, an avant-garde California band that featured Ry Cooder for a time and worked on several projects with Frank Zappa.

if you want to be a bird

We kept changing our name to come up with something that people would call us back. We were the Total Modal Rounders and then somebody got hold of some pot and thought "Total" was "Holy" and that name stuck. Our whole thing was we thought folk music in the 1960s was taking itself way too seriously. We wanted to get back to the 1920s and 1930s when you had groups like the Fruit Jar Drinkers and the Home Hair Pullers. They were having fun, and that's what we wanted to do.

We got with the Fugs, who knew nothing about music, but were very good at writing raunchy songs about sex and drugs. I got into that because I felt very strongly about liberating the language. Lenny Bruce was destroyed and all for saying a few cuss words.

When I look back on the '60s, it was more fun than I thought could be had. I thought rock died out in the late 1950s, but then the Beatles and the other groups hit and the music came back like a phoenix. It surpassed what anybody could even have dreamed of.

PETER STEMPFEL played banjo and fiddle for the Holy Modal Rounders. Their "If You Want To Be a Bird" appeared on the *Easy Rider* soundtrack. Their "Boobs a Lot" got a lot of airplay on FM. The Rounders worked in folk circles and recorded with the Fugs. Stempfel continues to perform, but is also an associate editor of a publishing company.

sunday will never be the same

We had a good run from 1966 until 1969 when we agreed to stop while we still had a good name. Two members died [Malcolm Hale and Lefty Baker] and that was a factor. We sold 13 million records and that was pretty good.

I met Spanky [McFarlane] at Mom's in Coconut Grove. She went to Chicago, but told me to look her up if I ever got there. My bass player at the time made threats against LBJ. Somebody heard what he said and turned his name in. We had to get out of town, so we headed to Chicago. We waited until Malcolm got out of Vietnam and then we started putting the group together.

Did Spanky and Our Gang make me wealthy? Hell, no. I don't have a pot to piss in. That's what money is for. You spend it. I bought everything I could get my hands on. I don't miss it at all. I live comfortably on a pension, Social Security and Humana. I don't pay nothing.

NIGEL PICKERING was a member of Spanky and Our Gang. The band scored with "Sunday Will Never Be The Same" and "Like To Get To Know You."

BLUES MAGOOS

I left home at the age of 14, hell-bent on being a rock-and-roll star. I was playing four sets a night, six nights a week at the Night Owl Café in Greenwich Village. One night, while rehearsing in the club, our brand new Echoplex, which cost a fortune when you're making $45 a week, fell off the piano and smashed onto the floor. We were crushed and bummed out. When we plugged it back into the amp, it was feeding back a sound that was like a train spinning in a tornado. Because it worked on the principle of a tape loop, when we moved the tape selector around, the speed of the sound would change.

We all flipped out and thought it was the coolest thing. Thus the psychedelic sound of the Blues Magoos was born. The owner of the club was used to us singing our catchy little songs. He thought we were doing fine until we went psychedelic. One night, we were really wigging out and getting into it and he starts flashing the lights on and off and we're thinking, wow, Joe is really getting into it, too. At the end of the set, we realized Joe was trying to tell us to get off the stage and end the set.

He told us we were too loud and fired us. Six months later, we had the No. 2 record in the country.

PEPPY CASTRO was lead singer for the Blues Magoos, a psychedelic rock quintet from the Bronx. Their top-seller was "We Ain't Got Nothing Yet" in 1967.

we ain't got nothing yet

bend me, shape me

I stayed with the group from 1966 until 1969 when they changed directions and started calling themselves Ask Rufus, which was a precursor to Chaka Khan.

I consider that an excellent time in my life because we earned the respect of the musical community. I still remember getting my gold record on the *Joey Bishop Show.*

Bill Trout was our producer and he was always looking around for songs. He got wind of "Bend Me" and thought it would be good for our group. A band called Amen Corner covered it in England at about the same time, and it was nip-and-tuck with them for airplay. We ended up getting the better of things with sales of 2 million.

A lot of people don't know this, but Carole King submitted several songs to us, like "I Don't Think You Know Me At All" and "Don't Forget About Me." It was all due to Bill. He had quite a pull in the record business back then.

GARY LOIZZO (second from right at right, far right above) fronted the American Breed. Their "Bend Me, Shape Me" was one of the top-selling songs of 1967. These days, he oversees Pumpkin Recording Studio and is the head engineer for Styx.

AMERICAN BREED

could this be magic?

Richard Blandon, our lead singer, came up with "Magic" when he was singing with the Royal Robins in the Air Force. When he got out, he played it for us. We liked the song and, fortunately, it did well in the charts.

We went on some bus tours with people like Sam Cooke. We all enjoyed spiritual music and I have fond memories of singing gospel songs together in between shows.

Having said that, the Dubs had a big problem with drinking. We worried about giving a good performance and a shot or two gave us the courage we needed. Pretty soon, it started getting out of hand, although we never missed a show.

I left the group a time or two in the 1960s because I had to put bread on the table for my family. I became a shipping clerk and worked my way up to supervisor.

We still perform in New York, Pennsylvania and Canada. We added a girl singer and we've got a very explosive band. My only problem now is my legs. I slipped and hurt myself. Now I sing sitting down.

CLEVELAND STILL was a member of the Dubs, a rhythm-and-blues quintet that had a hit with "Could This Be Magic?" in 1957.

THE BLUES PROJECT

I have very pleasant memories of the Project. It was a time of stunning creativity and hope for a new generation. I think we helped pave the way for groups such as Cream because we showed the record companies that albums could sell without a hit single.

I'm proud that we weren't a kiss-ass band. We didn't want exposure at the risk of not being able to be ourselves. We never felt it was our job to try to consolidate our audience. As a result, we have devout fans in the New York City area, but it starts to thin out elsewhere.

When it comes to money, we were definitely exploited by management and accountants. We just had a good time. They were much hipper about the money — or so we thought — than the band was. When you're 20 years old, about the last thing you're thinking about is the tax man. Nobody wants to tell you what to do until you're depleted somewhat. If they don't, what's in it for them?

ANDY KULBERG played bass and flute for the Blues Project, a New York City-based band that helped start the blues revival in the late 1960s. Members included keyboardist Al Kooper and Steve Katz, who later played with Blood, Sweat & Tears. These days, Kulberg produces CDs of classical music and composes for films and advertising.

COOL GHOUL

dinner with drac

I was the host of a late-night horror show on WCAU-TV in Philadelphia. I would dress up in that kind of monster character with the makeup and everything and do little takeoffs on the movie. Bernie Lowe was the head of Cameo Records at the time and he saw the program with his little girl. Lowe knew Dick Clark and that's how I got the "Cool Ghoul" nickname.

A standard part of the show was me reciting limericks that people would send in about the horror films. Bernie got the idea to make a record of some of that material — you know, like "I choked on the wine when I learned the main course was me." The tune was a big hit and I ended up making about $10,000, which was good money back then, considering they didn't have much of a way to keep track of what came in.

The show later moved to New York. I went on Dick Clark's show several times, especially around Halloween. Later I did some parodies like "Spookalong with Zacherle," which was a takeoff on "Singalong with Mitch." Then I did a dance show that featured groups like the Doors and the Loving Spoonful when they were just starting out.

I'm still doing the "Cool Ghoul" thing at horror sci-fi conventions. Going along with that, we came out with a CD of all new songs called *Dead Man's Ball.*

JOHN ZACHERLE, aka the "Cool Ghoul," had a novelty hit with "Dinner With Drac" in 1958.

out of sight, out of mind

When I look back over the old days, I remember the racial prejudice that black groups had to endure. We were on a tour called the Big Show with Big Joe Turner, Little Richard and B.B. King. You'd perform one-nighters every day for three months or more. At some cities in the South, black performers were not allowed to play with whites, even if the whites

were in the group. In Sumter, South Carolina, the KKK was in the parking lot when we went into the auditorium. There was no violence, but they harassed us and burned some crosses.

But we got through it. One reason was that we were determined not to be stopped. And we felt we had something that was very important to pass on. That would be the music. It's an international language. Everybody understands it. We had a love of what we were doing and we had a love for people. And why wouldn't we love the people? They bought our records. What other reason would you need?

MARYLAND PIERCE (second from right at right, far right at left) sings with the Five Keys, a rhythm-and-blues quintet formed in Newport News, Virginia. Among their hits was "Out of Sight, Out of Mind" in 1956. Their first performance was in 1949.

FIVE KEYS

BRUCE TERGESEN

The Cream album was *Disraeli Gears*, and I worked with the late Felix Pappalardi (of Mountain fame). He was a spunky guy. He knew a lot about the music and we had a good time together, even though we were so technically limited back then. I remember that there was a lot of competition between Ginger Baker and Eric Clapton as to which one would be heard the loudest. We split Clapton on the left and Baker on the right, so they would be exactly the same. That way, if one of them called to complain, we would just say they must not have their stereo tuned right.

Jim Croce was a very settled, very down-to-earth person. He loved telling truck-driving stories. He'd kid around with us about how you should never stick your thumb in the steering wheel of a big rig. If you hit a big bump, you could get it dislocated. I remember he wrote a song called "Speedball Trucker." It was about how you should stay out of the way of tractor-trailers because the drivers might be on speed.

BRUCE TERGESEN was an engineer on records put out by Cream and Jim Croce, among others. He continues to do recording work, mostly with jazz.

good golly, miss molly

I was in Grenada, Mississippi, visiting my family when I heard from Bumps Blackwell, the A&R man. Little Richard was on his way to a recording session in New Orleans and Bumps wanted me to have a song for him. I couldn't think of a title. I went to the local radio station where I used to work and told the DJ I was stuck. We started talking about the kind of tune Bumps wanted and all of a sudden the DJ came out with "Good Golly, Miss Molly."

I knew the title would work. I got in my brother's car and drove around all of Sunday night until I had the song. Then I made arrangements to get on the City of New Orleans train so I could be at the recording session.

But Little Richard was being a rebel about it and didn't show up. It seems he wanted to use his own band. I was paying my own expenses, so I couldn't afford to stay forever. I went back to Mississippi. Little Richard came a few days later and put down the song. I missed out on being at the recording session, but I was happy with the way the record came out.

Songwriter JOHN MARASCALCO penned "Rip It Up," "Ready Teddy" and "Good Golly, Miss Molly."

JOHN MARASCALCO

i had too much to dream last night

being in the Electric Prunes was exciting, but there were too many personality clashes that took away from the fun. Jim Lowe [lead singer] was a control freak and it was his way or no way. He was always telling everybody how to play even if he didn't know anything about the instrument.

We got "Too Much to Dream" from songwriters Annette Tucker and Nancy Mantz. The demo was in ballad style with somebody like Al Martino singing the demo. We fiddled around with it and came up with a nice psychedelic twist that was the group's style.

Another reason why I left the group was because of Dave Hassinger, our producer. All the contracts came through him, and he was an absolute dictator. He wanted us to record stuff we had no interest in. He had us release this song called "Dr. Do-Good," which we didn't like at all. The flip side was "Hideaway," which we wrote. Critics have written that it would have been a hit because it had a beat like the Stones' "Paint It Black."

Money entered the picture also. The Electric Prunes are still selling records all over the world, but to this day group members haven't seen a cent of the money. I have a team of lawyers working on it, but I don't know if anything will come out of it.

PRESTON RITTER was the drummer for the Electric Prunes, a Los Angeles psychedelic band that had a 1966 hit with "I Had Too Much to Dream Last Night." He performed with Linda Ronstadt, James Brown and Neil Diamond before joining the Los Angeles Police Department. He then went to South Korea, where he worked in Christian ministry.

THE ELECTRIC PRUNES

barbara ann

When we were handed "Barbara Ann," it sounded a lot like "Hard-Headed Woman." We changed it around and added the falsetto and the bass and people in New York bought it like crazy. Soon sales were more than 3 million. A few years later, the Beach Boys covered it and the song became one of their bigger records.

I've been on the injured list for a few months, but I've kept the band together over the years. We do a lot of corporate work. We had a nice experience not long ago when they flew us and the Temptations out to Hawaii.

I look back on the early 1960s in a mixed way. If I didn't have a hit record, I would have been better off financially to have worked in private industry. We played six shows a day, seven days a week at the Brooklyn Paramount and all we got was $250 apiece. And we were the No. 1 group in the country. If you have a hit record today, you can retire. Back then? Forget about it.

The good thing about the music business was we were a bunch of 19-year-old kids and we were touring the country with people like Duane Eddy, doing things anybody would love to do. But if you really look at what happened, it ruins your life . . . sucks you into the vortex. I know a lot of people who became drug addicts and became useless. It was almost a crime what happened. The music wasn't worth that.

GUY VILLARI was the lead singer with the Regents, a Bronx vocal group that formed as the Desires in 1958. Their big hit was "Barbara Ann" in 1961.

LITTLE JOEY & THE FLIPS

Growing up, we sang a lot in parking buildings because the acoustics were so great. Men's rooms were good, too. There were singers everywhere. We'd hurry to the 69th Street Terminal at 4:30 in the afternoon to sing for rush hour. It was great practice for performing.

We worked in a lot of pool rooms — social clubs, they were called — and some people heard us and liked us. Little Joey [Hall] was doing gospel at that time. He wasn't part of our original group, but they introduced him to us and our harmonies worked out.

It was almost instant success. We went from street corner to hit record in a matter of weeks. I was only 16 and not ready at all for what happened behind the music. It's a whole other scene.

We ended up going to court over "Bongo Stomp." Our managers felt we were too young to record in our own names, so they put their names on it. We sold something like 800,000 copies, but we only got about $10,000 apiece. We made more money doing TV shows.

The group lasted until some of us got drafted. I came back from Vietnam in 1965, but we never could find Joey, so that was it for the singing. We went to college so we could get a regular paycheck like everybody else. The Flips happened so very long ago. I don't even have any of our records. Just tapes.

FRED GERACE sang first tenor for Philadelphia-based Little Joey and the Flips, who charted with "Bongo Stomp" in 1963. Today, he works in bridge and road construction.

bongo stomp

While I studied classical piano from the age of 5, I never had a thought of pursuing music as a profession until 1963, when I took a course in it at the University of Santa Barbara in southern California. There was a kid in the dorm with a Fender Jazzmaster guitar and a big Standel amplifier. He could only play simple surf music and was clearly more interested in the effect this music had on the girls than the possibilities suggested by the electric guitar. It dawned on me that anything he could do, I could do better, despite the fact I had never played the guitar in my life.

When I got back home, I asked my dad if I could have the old Harmony F-hole acoustic guitar he had taken with him in the service. Then I invested $24 in a DeArmond pickup and another $85 in an old Fender tweed amp. I only played lead, using my well-developed ear and theory to learn the necessary lines from records. By Christmas of that year, I had formed a surf band and we played school dances. I also became a promoter, renting an old skating rink, hiring security and making the posters.

In 1966, I packed my belongings and moved to the San Francisco Bay area. During the next three years I had a variety of adventures and lived in a dozen places. About half that time was devoted to a rock group called the Indian Head Band. We featured a female opera singer and myself on lead guitar. My hair grew to a two-foot cascade of red gold curls and waves.

I heard the fledgling It's A Beautiful Day in their inaugural show at the Fillmore. They had a striking lyrical sound when David LaFlamme played, but as soon as he put down the violin to sing, the sound thinned to a muddy, ill-defined wash. The band had no guitarist. I shouldered my way through the crowd and had a brief conversation with David. I outlined my training and suggested the band let me work with them for a week.

They decided I was just what they needed. The combination of classical background and underground psychedelic jamming experience was a perfect fit — ideas flowing from Linda (David's wife), presented by David, arranged by me and supported by all.

This was 1969. We signed with CBS and spent a long time in Los Angeles recording our debut album, which was released the following year.

The music achieved broad success in America

and Europe, but the seeds of destruction had been planted. Linda left the band and David refused to continue the group approach and wanted to do only his songs. Since Linda had been the creator of most of the song concepts, the music rapidly disintegrated into mediocrity. David remained on his high horse and I left during the recording of our third album.

HAL WAGENET survived a sawmill accident that almost severed his fingers and relearned how to play the guitar. These days, he continues to operate the family's sawmill business. He also has a recording studio and operates a sound and lighting company.

east-west

At the University of Chicago in 1962 and 1963, we had something called the Twist Party. It was a Wednesday-night affair that started as a dormitory record party. When musicians and bands started showing up, it moved to the ballroom of nearby Ida Noyes Hall. The twist parties drew revelers from both the campus world and the adjacent Southside neighborhoods, which made for a nice social mix. It was in this milieu that I first heard Paul Butterfield, whose ensemble, with Elvin Bishop on guitar, became the house band. Their rocking blues excited me and awaked a keen longing. Sometimes I jumped in (uninvited) on piano.

Like everyone else who heard Paul in Chicago, I was captivated by his virtuosity as a blues harp player. But in early 1965, when I moved to New York City and the ensemble — now officially the Paul Butterfield Blues Band — made its Big Apple debut, I was stunned by his artistic greatness. His performance at the Village Gate was a revelation. He built his songs as sonic edifices, alternating sections of sung and played verses, powerfully lifting the music with each new entrance of harp. Later that year, he inducted me into the ensemble, and so for several years of club dates and concerts I stood with him on stage and felt his music, which was so heartbroken that one note could tear you up.

Paul Butterfield's artistry has inspired me from then until now.

MARK NAFTALIN (second from left) played keyboards for the Paul Butterfield Blues Band. The group performed at the Monterey Pop Festival that featured Janis Joplin as well as the Monterey Jazz Festival where they shared billing with the Jefferson Airplane. These days he operates Winner Records.

PAUL BUTTERFIELD BLUES BAND

uh oh

I was a music director for McCann-Erickson, an advertising agency in New York City. Being in charge of music written and produced for many of the agency's clients, I had occasion to hire Don Elliot, whom I had heard in the George Shearing Quintet.

We became quite friendly and frequently worked after hours at Nola Studios, writing and arranging original material with a rhythm section Don was using in concerts. We had Jack Six on bass, Ronnie Bedford on drums and Don Arnone and George Barnes on guitars.

We wrote a couple of pieces we thought could be pop hits and even had some released. But then one day we were talking about the Chipmunks and the half-speed overdubbing technique which pushed voices up an octave. We liked the technical aspect that forced us to work with clarity and pitch over half-speed music tracks, but we hated the kind of material the Chipmunks recorded. We thought we would write and record a newer, hipper version and try to get young listeners interested in jazz.

Thus the Nutty Squirrels were born. We took our first two efforts — "Uh, Oh, Parts 1 and 2" — to Milton DeLugg at Hanover Records. The masters were bought on the spot, quickly released and to our surprise became the fastest selling single in the country for the first eight weeks of being in the market.

An album followed, consisting of a mix of originals and jazz standards by Thelonius Monk and others. Because of the success of the Nutty Squirrels, an album for Columbia called *Birdwatching* followed with more originals and standards like "Skylark," with big orchestra accompaniment. It was a very good album and I still meet people who remember it with affection from their kidhood.

MGM released a third album of the Nutty Squirrels doing pop hits by Roy Orbison and the Beatles. It was a good album, but the driving jazz feeling wasn't there.

SASCHA BURLAND was a member of the Nutty Squirrels, a novelty group in the late 1950s. Today, he does cartoon work and paints landscapes.

tom dooley

We were rehearsing in a loft above the Purple Onion in San Francisco when we heard this old fellow auditioning downstairs. His song was "Tom Dooley." We were just starting out, not even a group yet. We thought it would be a good song for us, so we put it in.

We had no idea it would take off like it did. We considered it just another song on our album.

But these disc jockeys in Salt Lake City saw it as an alternative to the teenybopper craze that was going on. They played the tune a lot and told all their DJ friends about it. Everything came together and "Tom Dooley" became quite successful.

BOB SHANE (far left at right, center above) is a member of the Kingston Trio, which continues to tour 30 week s a year.

THE KINGSTON TRIO

see you in september

It's the summer of 1970 and we're booked for one night at a large night club in New Hampshire. While setting up that afternoon, the club owner came up to me with a problem. He said he wanted to put our hits on the marquee, but there wasn't enough room to fit them all. So I suggested he put, "The Happenings Sing Their Million Sellers." He agreed and assigned the job to a young kid who was cleaning up there. We went back to the hotel to shower and then headed back to the club that night. When we got to the club, the marquee read, "The Happenings Sing in Million Cellars." I probably have sung in that many, but I wondered how he knew.

Two years before, we had just finished a concert in St. John, New Brunswick. Rich Little opened for us and was supposed to do 40 minutes. He did two hours. What a ham. Anyway, two of us — myself and Tom Guiliano — had to get back to New York City for an Army reserve meeting the next day. We had missed a couple and couldn't miss this one.

The weather was awful. Very cold and lots of ice and snow. No planes were leaving. We decided to hire a private plane to get us at least to Boston and then we could catch something to New York. We did. It was a twin-engine Cessna with a pilot and co-pilot. We took off from Boston in the dark and in the snow. I kept noticing the co-pilot checking the wings with a flashlight. I asked about it and he said in a shaky

voice that there was a lot of ice building up on the wings and the plane was having trouble keeping altitude. In other words, we were getting closer and closer to the ocean.

I knew we were in trouble when the co-pilot started crying. I mean, really weeping. For some strange reason, I found this situation absolutely hysterical. I couldn't stop laughing and Tom started laughing, too. The combination of laughter and tears in that close little cockpit was one of the bizarre moments of my life.

Obviously, we made it to Boston, but I have never since then taken a small plane. And I never will.

BOB MIRANDA (far right at left, center above) was the lead singer for the Happenings, who had hits with "See You in September" and "I Got Rhythm." The group continues to perform.

THE HAPPENINGS

mr. custer

I was heavily involved in the Beach Boys' "Pet Sounds." Brian [Wilson] was very particular with his work. We would never work on more than one song at a session, and with "Good Vibrations" we worked on two different parts of the song at two different studios. Brian would come in with his ideas written on a piece of paper. We'd review what he had in mind and then start playing.

I was with Glen [Campbell] on "Wichita Lineman" and those big pop songs he had in the '60s. When those hits started to die down, I said he should retreat to country until we could hit again with a crossover. The label [Capitol] didn't like that idea. Their feeling was that we should keep going with the pop tonnage for as long as it would last. That's the way Glen felt about it, too. I ended up being let go as his producer. As success grows, the power of politics grows. There never was a big falling out. I just never got back.

Still, the biggest thing I ever did was "Custer." I do some speaking at music seminars. I'll play the first 16 bars and people still get a big charge out of it 40 years later.

AL DELORY helped write the novelty hit, "Mr. Custer," for Larry Verne. He played piano and keyboards for the Beach Boys and recorded with Phil Spector. He won two Grammy Awards as producer for Glen Campbell. These days, he performs with a nine-piece salsa band.

THE CHIMES

We started out singing on the corner of Fulton and Rockaway. We'd sing in the subway a lot because of the echo-chamber effect. There were tons of groups back then just like us, listening to Alan Freed and rapping with each other.

My dad was an accordion player and knew a lot of songs. We were looking for something to record, and he suggested we try "Once in a While." We made the demo and they told us to stick around. This guy from Tag Records came by and signed us to a contract. Six months later, that song was in the Top Ten. They had us follow that one with "I'm in the Mood for Love," but it fell flat.

I have very pleasant memories of that period of time. We toured with the Capris, Ray Hamilton and Moms Mabley to places like Chicago, Detroit and Montreal. Moms was a fantastic lady. When we played the Apollo Theater, she brought in caterers to feed everybody in all the groups.

I was still singing until 1999 when I suffered a stroke. I'm getting better, but I won't get back to singing.

LEONARD COCCO fronted the Chimes, a Brooklyn-based vocal quartet that charted with "Once in a While" in 1961.

i'm in the mood for love

© John Byrne Cook

I made my first washtub bass in 1954. Although I had never seen one, the name seemed self-explanatory. I used a wash-boiler, a hockey stick and a clothesline. By 1960, as an Army helicopter mechanic, I discovered stainless steel flight control cable and liberated yards and yards of it — in used condition but good enough for folk music — and made a much better instrument.

When I went back to Cambridge in 1962, the music scene was flowering. My friend Paul Rothchild, board member of Club 47, started recording the local acts, beginning with the Charles River Valley Boys, a group I was in. Paul moved to New York City, got a job at Elektra Records, and I was soon commuting to recording sessions there as he continued his series of folk albums. On one of these sessions, I met an enthusiastic harmonica player named John Sebastian. John loved jug band music and sought work with us in the Kweskin Band, but we already had two harmonica players. We were a bunch of people who loved to play music. We never had a hit record, so there was never any serious money. We could pay the rent and eat, but there wasn't enough for cars or real estate.

Kweskin disbanded, and Paul Rothchild, now a rock and roll producer, helped me get an interview at Elektra West Coast, which had just built a recording studio. I worked as second engineer on all sessions in that studio, including three Doors albums, and was engineer on three John Sebastian albums. One of my jobs with the Doors was to keep some of Jim Morrison's friends out of the studio because they'd all get drunk. Jim was useless when he had too much booze, but in the mornings he was an outgoing and engaging person. His eyes crackled with energy, yet he was always willing to chat and would listen to what a person had to say until the bottle showed up.

FRITZ RICHMOND played the jug and washtub bass for the Jim Kweskin Jug Band, a group that included Geoff and Maria Muldaur for a time. After the Kweskin Band broke up in 1968, he worked as a recording engineer for 20 years before becoming a legal assistant for a law firm. He continues to perform with John Sebastian and the J-Band.

city of angels

Shortly after "City of Angels" came out on Bally, the band auditioned for the *Arthur Godfrey Talent Scouts* show. We passed the audition in Chicago and, a week later, were told we had to fly to New York to appear on

the Monday night show. None of us had ever flown before.

We got to Midway Airport in Chicago and found our way to the Capitol Records departure gate. In those days, we still had to go out on the tarmac and climb the moving ramp. The weather was overcast and the flight was delayed. After we finally took off, we found out that it was going to be a four-hour flight. We ran out of magazines to read and started to get a little nervous about our first television show.

One of the stewardesses noticed that we were all dressed alike, and asked us where we were going. We told her about our record and our appearance on the Godfrey Show, and she asked us if we would sing something. It was a good way to relax, so we started to go through all the songs we knew. Other passengers requested songs and we did those, too, making it up as we went along.

We must have sung for two hours, and enjoyed the opportunity to rehearse and entertain. As we got off the plane, all the stewardesses met us at the door and thanked us for keeping the passengers calm because for the final hour we had been in a holding pattern at the tail end of Hurricane Flossie. We all turned a few shades of green as we got off the plane on very wobbly knees. What a

first flight for four guys who were still in high school.

FRANK CALZARETTA (far left in both pictures) was a member of the Highlights, who had a hit with "City of Angels" in 1956. These days, he works as an executive recruiter.

THE HIGHLIGHTS

miserlou

My father's family came from Beirut, Lebanon. As a kid, I can remember hearing "Miserlou" being played on a musical instrument called an *oud,* which looks a lot like a lyre. What I did was put a jet engine afterburner on the tune.

The sound I was after was the tribal drumming of Gene Krupa like at a fertility dance. To make the song sound big and full I had to speed it up.

When people ask what did Dick Dale really do, I would say that beginning in 1955 I changed the technology of rock and roll. That was the jazz era. You didn't play loud. You didn't play powerfully. It was the Les Paul style. Soft. Eloquent. Nice.

I'm the guy who made people's ears bleed. I'm not a guitar player as much as I'm a manipulator of instruments. I couldn't get the sound I wanted, so I kept blowing up amplifiers and catching speakers on fire. When we finally got it right, that's how we created the power amps of the world.

DICK DALE, billed as the "King of Surf Guitar," pioneered a heavily reverbed guitar style that influenced the Beach Boys. His best-known songs are "Miserlou" and "Surf Beat." He continues to tour.

DICK DALE

photo credits

Pages 5, 15, 32–33, 36, 69, MICHAEL OCHS ARCHIVES.COM

Page 28, © Sherry Rayn Barnett / MICHAEL OCHS ARCHIVES.COM

Pages xii-xiii, 8, 128, AP/Wide World Photos

Page 113, This is a HONOLULU STAR-BULLETIN PHOTO

All other photographs are property of and were supplied by the artists.

index of bands

1910 Fruitgum Company, 43

American Breed, 92

Association, The, 61

Black Oak Arkansas, 35

Blues Magoos, 91

Blues Project, The, 95

Captain Beefheart and the Magic Band, 88

Champs, The, 7

Chantays, The, 62

Chimes, The, 117

Cleftones, The, 38

Cool Ghoul, 96

Country Joe & the Fish, 2

Danny and the Juniors, 76

Diamonds, The, 10

Dubs, The, 94

Electric Prunes, The, 102

Elephant's Memory, 85

Fireballs, The, 24

Five Keys, 98

Flamin' Groovies, The, 12

Grass Roots, The, 22

Happenings, The, 114

Harper's Bizarre, 52

Harptones, The, 54

Herman's Hermits, 64

Highlights, The, 120

Holy Modal Rounders, 89

Ides of March, The, 40

It's a Beautiful Day, 106

Jaggerz, 20

Jim Kweskin Jug Band, 118

Johnny and the Hurricanes, 56

Joy of Cooking, The, 16

Kingsmen, The, 14

Kingston Trio, The, 112

Lemon Pipers, 59

Little Anthony and the Imperials, 68

Little Joey and the Flips, 105

Majors, The, 41

Mason Williams, 66

"Mr Custer," 30

New Colony Six, The, 18

Nutty Squirrels, The, 110

Ohio Express, 70

Paul Butterfield Blues Band, 108

Playmates, The, 42

Randy and the Rainbows, 82

Rare Earth, 19

Regents, The, 104

Sam the Sham and the Pharaohs, 32

Seeds, The, 8

Sha Na Na, 80

Shadows of Night, The, 34

Soul Survivors, 47

Spanky and Our Gang, 90

Sugarloaf, 50

Surfaris, The, 48

Tokens, The, 6

Weavers, The, 74

index of artists

Austin, Sil, 78
Bratton, Creed, 22
Browne, Ivan, 59
Burland, Sascha, 110
Calzaretta, Frank, 120
Castro, Peppy, 91
Cita, Raoul, 54
Cocco, Leonard, 117
Conn, Donny, 42
Conniff, Ray, 72
Dale, Dick, 122
Delory, Al, 116
Felts, Narvel, 26
Forte, Fabian, 37
Garthwaite, Terry, 16
Gerace, Fred, 105
Gottehrer, Richard, 51
Gourdine, Anthony, 68
Graffia, Ray, 18
Harkleroad, Bill, 88
Hellerman, Fred, 74
Ingui, Richard, 47
Jaye, Jerry, 86
Jeckell, Frank, 43
Kastran, Dean, 70
Kulberg, Andy, 95
Loizzo, Gary, 92
Loney, Ray, 12
MacKendrick, Keith, 7
MacVittie, Bob, 50
Mangrum, Jim Dandy, 35
Marascalco, John, 101
Marcellino, Jocko, 80
Margo, Phil, 6
Maybray, William, 20
Melton, Barry, 2
Metis, Frank, 60
Millas, Larry, 40
Miranda, Bob, 114
Naftalin, Mark, 108
Noone, Peter, 64
Pash, Jim, 48
Patterson, Berman, 38
Paxton, Tom, 28
Peterson, Dick, 14
Pickering, Nigel, 90
Pierce, Maryland, 98
Platt, Eddie, 84
Richmond, Fritz, 118
Ritter, Preston, 102
Rivera, Peter, 19
Rivers, Johnny, 4
Sainte-Marie, Buffy, 9
Samudio, Domingo, 32
Savich, Bo, 56
Saxon, Sky, 8
Schiffour, Tom, 34
Scoppetone, Dick, 52
Shane, Bob, 112
Somerville, David, 10
Spickard, Bob, 62
Starr, Kay, 71
Stempfel, Peter, 89
Still, Cleveland, 94
Tergesen, Bruce, 100
Terry, Joe, 76
Tomsco, George, 24
Troutt, Frank, 41
Van Dyke, Leroy, 44
Verne, Larry, 30
Villari, Guy, 104
Wagenet, Hal, 106
Williams, Mason, 66
Yester, Jim, 61
Yules, Myron, 85
Zacherle, John, 96
Zero, Mike, 82